Value Stream Mapping for Lean Development

A How-To Guide for Streamlining Time to Market

Value Stream Mapping for Lean Development

A How-To Guide for Streamlining Time to Market

Drew A. Locher

CRC Press
Taylor & Francis Group
Boca Raton   London   New York

CRC Press is an imprint of the
Taylor & Francis Group, an **informa** business

A PRODUCTIVITY PRESS BOOK

Productivity Press
Taylor & Francis Group
270 Madison Avenue
New York, NY 10016

© 2008 by Taylor & Francis Group, LLC
Productivity Press is an imprint of Taylor & Francis Group, an Informa business

---

Library of Congress Cataloging-in-Publication Data

Locher, Drew.
   Value stream mapping for lean development: a how-to guide for streamlining time to market / Drew A. Locher.
       p. cm.
   Includes bibliographical references and index.
   ISBN 978-1-56327-372-8 (alk. paper)
   1. New products. 2. Time to market (New products) I. Title.

TS170.L63 2008
658.5'75--dc22   2007050906

Visit the Taylor & Francis Web site at
http://www.taylorandfrancis.com

and the Productivity Press Web site at
http://www.productivitypress.com

Contents

Acknowledgments ix

Introduction xi

1   Applying Value Stream Mapping to the Development Process 1

2   What Makes the Development Process Different? 9

3   Identifying Development Waste 15

4   Assessing the Current State 23

5   Developing a Current State Map for DevelopTek 35

6   Lean Development Principles... 45

7   Creating the Future State Map 55

8   DevelopTek's Future State 77

9   Achieving the Future State.. 89

Appendix 97

Index 123

Dedication

This book is dedicated to Eileen. Thank you for your love and support over the years, as well as the confidence that you have shown in me. It has not been easy with the travel and stress, but knowing that I am coming home to you seems to make it all okay. I am "Lucky" to have you.

And, as always, to those with whom I have worked — you are the true innovators.

Acknowledgments

As I reflect on the past and decide whom to acknowledge for contributions to this book, as well as my career as an agent for change in business, I continue to return to the General Electric Company. GE provided me with a wealth of experience and knowledge in the 1980s that I continue to discover over twenty years later was quite ahead of its time. In 1986, we developed a methodology called Integrated Product and Process Development. Today we call it Lean Product Development. While the titles have changed, the underlying methodologies have not and for good reason; they have proven to work time and time again. The difficulty is in getting organizations to apply them.

To that end, I would like to thank James Womack and Daniel Jones who continue to lead the way in challenging people and organizations to fundamentally change the way they think about business. With their writings and speeches, they often are responsible for that first opening of the mind that gives the rest of us an opportunity to show an organization the way forward. I would also like to thank John Shook and Michael Rother for being the first to document the value stream mapping methodology. VSM is not just a tool, it is a practical means by which to teach Lean thinking and how it applies to any process, including the development process.

I would like to thank Productivity Press for their continued support to expand the body of knowledge of Lean thinking. Thanks to Maura May, Michael Sinocchi, and Lara Zoble, as well as my editor Kirsten Miller who made the editing process a true collaboration and a quite enjoyable one.

Introduction

For at least twenty years, organizations in a number of different industries have subscribed to a common rule of thumb—that every dollar correction on the proverbial drawing board can cost as much as *one thousand dollars* if left uncorrected and discovered by the customer. The cost of correcting a product or service failure increases incrementally (as much as tenfold) as it proceeds through each major stage of development, from concept to the customer (Figure I.1). Although the specific dollar amounts may vary based on the particular product or service, the point remains: Poor design and development processes can add significant cost to any business.

In addition, most industries now experience significant pressure to reduce the lead time to market for new products and services. As organizations face increasing competition, speed to market can become not only the key differentiator (the thing that sets one organization apart from the next), but also the key to survival. For example, in the automotive industry, increased demand for new models and other market trends (such as higher gas prices) mean that traditional thirty-eight- to forty-eight-month product development lead times are no longer acceptable. Today, the industry leader, Toyota, posts development lead times of fifteen months on average, and as low as ten to thirteen months on some projects. The downward pressure on lead time can be still greater for service organizations, as it is often easier in these industries for consumers to change service providers. As a result, service organizations, such as call centers, help lines, or technical

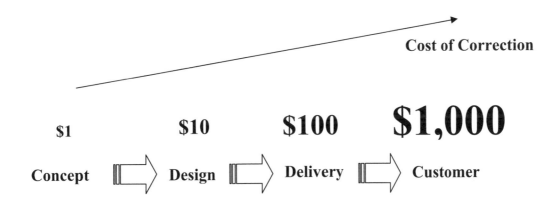

Figure I.1   The "rule of tens."

support centers, must also be prepared to quickly redesign their processes to respond to ever-changing market conditions.

The world is changing quickly, consumer expectations are high, and companies must be quick to adapt if they are to survive and thrive. Organizations need proven concepts for reducing lead time—and the tools to do so—if they are to remain competitive. Lean development is one such tool.

Lean is defined as a systematic approach to maximizing value by minimizing waste, and by flowing the product or service at the pull of the customer demand. These key concepts of "value," "flow," and "pull," align with the ultimate Lean goal: "perfection," or a continuous striving for improvement in the performance of the organization. The typical benefits of the successful application of Lean include greatly reduced lead times of 40 to 90 percent, reduced process times of 30 to 50 percent, and improved quality performance of 30 to 70 percent.

Given these results, why is it that so many companies have yet to tackle their development processes and to apply proven Lean concepts to them? The answer may lie in the nature of the development process. Some organizations claim that high variability in the development process is the reason that "development is different," and is why "Lean does not apply." In these organizations, often the lead time and amount of effort necessary to complete the development process can vary greatly from project to project. The naysayers believe, then, that Lean only applies to repetitive processes, such as the manufacture of standard products. However, this is not the case. Too often the root causes of this variability are left unaddressed, with the rationale that they are a natural part of the creative process. These numerous and actionable root causes, if addressed, can greatly reduce process variability, decrease waste, and improve flow. These are just some of the benefits that Lean offers.

Another reason for the reluctance to implement Lean may be the nature of the people involved in the development process—the knowledge workers—and a fear of hindering their creativity by instituting standard work procedures and other Lean concepts. The majority of product or service development involves understanding what information is needed, where the information can be obtained, and what to do with it once it is in hand. This all involves process, and processes can be streamlined and standardized using Lean concepts. In turn, once these processes have been streamlined, organizations often find that they have *more* time for truly creative activities. Unfortunately, it can be difficult for knowledge workers to immediately recognize this opportunity. Often, it requires a "leap of faith" on their part to even consider the application of Lean.

Furthermore, there are few published examples on which novices can draw experience and confidence. Although there are numerous books on the subject of product development, most tend to focus on the myriad development-related tools (e.g., design for manufacturability), or promote sequential, gate-based processes. (These concepts are covered at length in the book.) Lost in many of these books are the key principles upon which a Lean development process is based. In fact, the success of Toyota's development process, which is among the forerunners of Lean development, has only recently been documented in *The Toyota Product Development System* by James Morgan and Jeffrey Liker (2006). In it, the authors identify thirteen key principles, organized by three categories: process, tools and technology, and skilled people. These concepts will be discussed in detail in the book.

Lean Note

The original Lean concept of "flow" dates back to around 1910 and is attributed primarily to Henry Ford. Toyota, however, is credited with taking Ford's original flow concepts to the next level, with diversified small lot production. While not specifically using the term *Lean*, Toyota has applied Lean concepts for more than fifty years to its production and product development systems and is widely recognized as the leader in the application of Lean thinking. In 1990, James Womack and Daniel Jones documented the success of the Toyota Production System (TPS) in *The Machine that Changed the World*. Womack and Jones went on to demonstrate that it represents a fundamentally different way of thinking about processes, systems, and organizations as a whole when they published *Lean Thinking* in 1996.

But, what is still missing from the literature is a "how-to" book. *How* can organizations get their arms around an often poorly defined existing development process and redesign it based on the concepts of Lean thinking? To start, they need a reference to guide them through a step-by-step methodology that they can apply, in a real-time, practical way, to their own development processes.

This book provides that methodology. In it, we focus on process and system principles, as well as specific people principles strongly related to process. Our primary focus on process and system principles does not in any way mean that the people principles are less important. On the contrary, these principles are often—and wrongly—overlooked. However, to allow for the practical application and implementation of Lean concepts to the development process, we must narrow our focus. Further, it is not the intention of this book to cover any of the specific development tools in any great depth. Brief descriptions of the more important tools are provided in the Appendix and can be referred to as needed.

Why do we use value stream mapping as the methodology? Value stream mapping is a method of visualizing the flow of a service, a product, or information. It provides a system's view of the flow of work, involving multiple processes, that goes well beyond traditional process mapping techniques. Through the use of symbols or icons, it conveys a great deal of information in a succinct manner. Also, it incorporates process and system-related data to further increase the power of the mapping methodology. As such, value stream mapping is *the* assessment and planning tool of Lean practitioners, and an enabling tool to apply Lean thinking.

We hope that *Value Stream Mapping for Lean Development: A How-To Guide for Streamlining Time to Market* is to *The Toyota Product Development System* (Morgan and Liker, 2006) what *Learning to See* (Rother and Shook, 1997) and *The Complete Lean Enterprise* (Keyte and Locher, 2004) are to *Lean Thinking* (Womack and Jones, 1996)—practical how-to guides with well-worn copies on the shelves of readers everywhere.

To accomplish this objective, we have created a case study (DevelopTek) to serve as a guide through the value stream mapping methodology. We will follow DevelopTek as they document existing development processes and redesign them based on Lean concepts. DevelopTek will accomplish its redesign through the application of seven prescriptive questions—the future state questions—that embody Lean thinking and the key concepts of value, flow, pull, and perfection. Although the specifics of the case study are meant to resonate with the reader, these details are not our primary focus. The case study simply provides a context around which a dialogue can take place.

In addition, throughout the book there will be

■ **Lean Notes**, which expand upon specific Lean concepts.
■ **Mapping Tips** to help the reader in the application of the value stream mapping tool to the development process.
■ **Lean Examples** or descriptions of particular applications from actual companies.

All are intended to provide readers and the companies they represent with the tools and confidence to tackle their development processes, and to create truly Lean development processes.

References

Keyte, B. and Locher, D. (2004) *The Complete Lean Enterprise*, Productivity Press, New York, NY.

Morgan, J. and Liker, J. (2006) *The Toyota Product Development System*, Productivity Press, New York, NY.

Rother, M. and Shook, J. (1997) *Learning to See*, Lean Enterprise Institute, Brookline, MA.

Womack, J. and Jones, D. (1991) *The Machine that Changed the World*, Harper-Collins, New York.

Womack, J. and Jones, D. (1996) *Lean Thinking*, FREE Press, New York, NY.

Chapter 1

Applying Value Stream Mapping to the Development Process

In *Lean Thinking* (1996), James Womack and Daniel Jones identified the three critical management tasks of any business:

1. Problem solving (e.g., product or service design)
2. Information management (e.g., order processing and other transactional activities)
3. Physical transformation (e.g., converting raw materials to finished product)

The authors define a value stream as the set of all specific actions required to bring a specific product or service through the critical management tasks. Clearly, there is a strong relationship among the three. For example, a product design that is difficult to build will negatively impact the "physical transformation" value stream. Also, poor information management from the market will negatively impact the "problem solving" value stream. Therefore, in manufacturing, all three ultimately must be addressed. For service organizations, the first two must be taken on.

Mike Rother and John Shook's landmark book, *Learning to See* (1998), was the first publication on the subject of value stream mapping. In *Learning to See,* the authors detailed value stream mapping's application to manufacturing (i.e., physical transformation). *The Complete Lean Enterprise* by Beau Keyte and Drew Locher (2004) extended value stream mapping's application to office and administrative processes (i.e., information management). Value stream mapping is an effective and proven tool to assess existing business processes and to re-design them based on "Lean" concepts. It is the intent of this book to address the problem solving critical management task or value stream.

As with all tools, there is a recommended process for using value stream mapping (Figure 1.1). The first step in the process—the "preparation" step—is

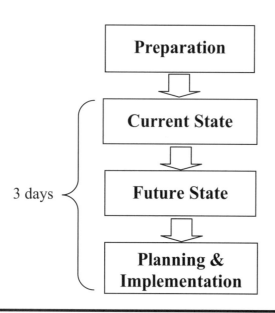

- Identifying the mapping team, the product or project to study, and how the project or product will be mapped.

- Agreeing on a well understood map of the current situation.

- Agreeing on a shared vision of a lean development process.

- Developing a plan to achieve the future state.

Figure 1.1   The value stream mapping process.

critical to conducting an effective value stream mapping event, and to the successful implementation of the envisioned "future state"; the preparation step occurs *before* the mapping event itself. During the preparation step, the team tasked with the objective of improving the development process is assembled. Next, this team develops the "current state"—a visual, agreed upon depiction of how things work today. The team then develops the future state—their shared vision of a new, Lean development process. Finally, there is the "planning and implementation" step.

The ultimate goal to value stream mapping is to achieve the future state and to realize the expected benefits. The typical duration of the mapping event is three days, including the development of the current state, the future state, and a detailed implementation plan. Obviously, implementation will occur after the event, over a one- to twelve-month period of time.

Mapping Tip

A value stream mapping (VSM) event involves a cross-functional team of participants, led by a value stream manager, who perform the various tasks throughout the value stream. The team will define the current process (i.e., the current state) using the VSM methodology described later in this book. Next, the team will use Lean concepts to re-design the current process and improve its performance (i.e., develop the future state), and will create a plan for implementing the new process. The typical three-day duration for a developmental VSM event should be considered a guideline. However, certain factors may create the need for more (or less) time. Three key factors that should be considered are the following:

- The level of definition that exists for the current process. Is the current process well documented? If not, you may want to provide additional time.
- The lead time of the current process. It may require more time to map a development process that spans four to five years, as opposed to one that requires one year to complete.
- Experience of the organization and the facilitator with value stream mapping.

In this chapter, we will describe the first step, preparation. We'll discuss the development of a current state map in chapter 4, and the development of a future state map in chapter 7. Planning and implementation will be discussed in chapter 9. Of course, **Mapping Tips** will be provided throughout this book.

Scoping the Effort

Some of the key questions that must be answered before the mapping event are

- What exactly will be mapped? What type of product, service or project?
- What processes will be included? Where or when will the map start and where or when will it end?
- Who needs to be on the mapping team? Who will be the value stream manager?
- What are the business objectives? What will be the measures of success?
- Who needs to support the effort? Who needs to be part of the decision process?
- What logistical plans need to be made to avoid difficulties that the mapping team may encounter?

In other words, the undertaking needs to be "scoped" during the preparation step. Proper scoping is critical to the success of the mapping event and to the success of the redesign effort itself. Because of this, managers who represent the functions or departments that are involved in the value stream must participate in the preparation step. These managers will identify the value stream mapping team and establish the guidelines that the team will follow. In all likelihood, they will also be part of the decision process regarding the future state and implementation plan. In addition, they will select a value stream manager who will lead the effort to successfully implement the future state following the conclusion of the mapping event. The guidelines that the managers should consider are provided below.

Identifying Famlies

Identifying the specific product or service to be mapped, or more aptly, the *groups* of products or services to be mapped, is an important early task. These groups are often referred to as "families." Families are groups of products or services that share *similar* process steps, which are the main activities performed as part of the development process. Our intent at this stage is not to map departments or functions, but rather to map the *flow of information* that moves between and among departments. We must follow the information flow from the customer (i.e., defined needs), through its processing, and finally through the delivery of a solution to the customer in the form of a product or service. To do this, we need to clearly define the product or service "family": the specific product or service that will serve as the subject for the mapping event.

One tool that can help with this task is the product or service matrix, shown in Figure 1.2. In this simplified example, there are two families: A and B. A represents development projects that are really redesign efforts. B requires new research and development processes to be created and completed. Terms used to distinguish between the two are "knowledge reuse" and "knowledge creation." So, which family will be mapped? There are several considerations to take into account when making this selection:

■ Demand for each (A represents 90 percent of demand, B just 10 percent).
■ Future business objectives (the need for new technologies is greater).
■ Current problems facing the company (the turnaround time for redesign projects is unacceptable to the market).

What we learn from one product or service family can often be applied to other families, but the key is to keep the effort and the team focused by identifying which processes are "in-scope" (and will be included on the value stream map) and which are "out-of-scope" (and will not be included on the map).

Process Steps

Product / Service	Research	Develop	Re-design	Document
A			X	X
B	X	X		X

Figure 1.2 Product or service matrix.

Work content is another factor to consider when identifying product or service families. This is particularly true in the case of design-to-order or engineer-to-order companies where the frequency of development is relatively higher. If one development project requires ten hours to complete, while another requires one thousand hours to complete, perhaps there is more than one family within A or B.

Selecting a Project

Once the product "family" has been defined, along with the processes that will be included in the value stream map, the team will need to select a project or projects to serve as the subject or subjects for the mapping event. We should have a specific project or projects in mind as we walk through the process from end to end. For example, staff members will need to provide estimates of various process times. Therefore, it only makes sense to identify a project for people to contemplate as they provide the necessary data that will be part of the value stream map. So, what project or projects will we use? Certainly, we should use only those that have been recently completed; there's no need to go back through a decade or more of history. Consider identifying two projects, so that the team can identify and discuss the variability between projects.

> ### *Lean Note*
>
> Identification of product or service families can be the breakthrough event that finally allows people in an organization to recognize how "Lean" really does apply, and how it can lead to significant results. People can become overwhelmed by the variety of tasks that they are faced with or by the variation that can occur within a task. As one engineering manager asked, "How can you apply Lean to a design when one project requires forty hours and another takes four hundred?" Still another said, "How can you apply Lean when some of my people are designing products for aerospace, while others are designing products for commercial applications?" These statements reflect a common excuse why "Lean will not work in my company—we're too complicated." Developing the product or service matrix can help these people begin to see their operation through simpler eyes, which is critical if they are to recognize the opportunities that really exist. They will discover that the different projects require most, if not all, of the same process steps.
>
> Another way to help identify different product or service families is to look at things from a customer viewpoint. A service may have different customer needs to meet (e.g., the "output" or result or the level of "service"). By recognizing this fact, the team may find it easier to distinguish service families based on the different needs of different customers.

> ### *Lean Example*
>
> At one company, three different design families were identified based on market needs. One family required a turnaround time of twelve to sixteen weeks, while another required twenty-six to fifty-two weeks. A third required two years. Although the processing steps did differ among the three, it wasn't until the company viewed the design process in terms of the lead time to market that it was able to categorize its disparate products into families. As part of their future state design, they actually structured their entire business based on these three families.
>
> Still another company reorganized by "knowledge creation" and "knowledge reuse." Previously, the same resources had been used to develop projects of widely varying scopes and activities. This variability made things difficult for the staff performing the work to "shift" between multiple projects in process at any time as well as for management to manage the various projects. Once the company reorganized, they recognized the benefits of reducing this variability: more effective and efficient use of resources, easier-to-manage projects, and more predictable process performance. The company realized that they had been improperly organized before.

Be careful. If the projects vary too much in terms of the process steps required or the work content necessary to complete the project, we may be looking at two different product or service families. If possible, gather project related information and documentation ahead of time. Have it available for people's reference, if necessary. Such preparation will allow for the mapping event to run more smoothly.

The information gathered and the decisions made during the preparation step can be summarized in a single-page document referred to as a SIPOC (Supplier Input –Process Output–Customer) (Figure 1.3).

Toward the center of the SIPOC in Figure 1.3, the main process steps or activities performed in the development process are identified, beginning with the "supplier" and ending with the "customer." The specific inputs and outputs have been clearly identified. This will sufficiently "bound" the value stream map by defining the first and last process step, thereby clearly defining which steps or activities will be included on the map (in other words, activities in-scope) and which will not be included (activities "out-of-scope"). Once this is done, it is very easy to see who needs to join the mapping team. Their names have been listed toward the lower right side. Always consider including "suppliers" and "customers" in the process, if possible; the reasons for this will be discussed in greater detail in subsequent chapters. A team of six to ten members is typical.

DevelopTek Value Stream Mapping Project

Objectives:
To Improve existing Product Development Process

Goals:
Reduce Product Development Lead Time b   0
Reduce Warrant   osts b
Reduce Product Development Cost by 30%

Project Name: New Product Development Process
VS Manager: Joe Smith, Engineering Manager
Sponsor: Diane Jones, VP of Research & Development
Leadership Decision Panel: VP of Operations, Diane, VP of R&D, onnie, VP of inance, John, VP of Procurement

Workshop Dates:
October 21 to October 23, 2006

Workshop Location:
Main Building, Conference Room A

Suppliers:	Inputs:						Outputs:	Customers:
Tool Design Firms	Lead Time				**Start:** Design Concept	**End:** Release to Product		**External:**
	Capabilities						Quality Product	New Customer
	Quality tooling						Quality Product	Existing Customer
Material Suppliers	Lead Time			Product. Develop.	Develop. Prototype	Product. Validation		**Internal:**
	Capabilities						Completed Design	Production
	Quality parts & materials						Completed Design	Purchasing
Sales & Marketing	Customer Requirements						Estimated Cost	Cost Accounting
	- Price						Product Features	Sales & Marketing
	- Lead Time							
	- Quality Expectations							
	- Competitive Information							

Issues/Problems	Benefits:	In Scope:	Out of Scope:	Technology:	Participants:	Data to Collect:
Losing potential new business due to long product development time.	Estimated increase of $10MM in additional annual sales revenue.	Re-design of existing product New Product using existing technology	New products using new technology & requiring research	ACAD	Steve, Tool Engineer	Lead Times from previous projects.
				MRP BOMs	Bill, Design Engineer	
Losing repeat customers due to design quality issues.	Estimated decrease of $1MM in annual warranty costs.			Testing Software	Eileen, Design Engineer	Process Times from previous project
					Pat, Supplier A	Information Quality issues
					John, Supplier B	Warranty Information.
					Rick, Process Engineer	Cost information
					Jane, Test Engineer	
					Bob, Engineering Services	

Figure 1.3   An example of SIPOC.

Key specific objectives and measures have been identified and recorded in the upper left corner. The Decision or Leadership Panel has been identified toward the top of the page, along with the project name, and the value stream manager. Very importantly, toward the bottom are clear statements of what is in-scope and out-of-scope. This will prevent scope creep, which occurs when mapping teams drift beyond their initial charter. The example provided above is just one possible format. It is most important, regardless of the format used, to identify and visually display all of the key elements of the preparation activity described previously.

Finally, any logistical challenges need to be identified and addressed during the preparation step. For example, some processes may be performed at different locations. How will this be handled? Will people need to be brought in from other sites to participate on the team and/or the decision panel? If so, how will they have access to the information that they will need? Will it be possible for them to access the computer-based systems, tools, and databases that they normally use? Further, the mapping team should always physically walk through the flow whenever possible. Are there challenges that stand in the way of doing this?

Once these important decisions have been made and the SIPOC has been created, the mapping event can be scheduled. The next chapter will review some of the characteristics of the development process that make mapping difficult, and thereby make the application of Lean that much more important.

References

Keyte, B. and Locher, D. (2004) *The Complete Lean Enterprise*, Productivity Press, New York.

Rother, M. and Shook, J., (1998) *Learning to See*, Lean Enterprise Institute, Brookline, MA.

Womack, J. and Jones, D. (1996) *Lean Thinking*, Free Press, New York.

Chapter 2

What Makes the Development Process Different?

Organizations struggle mightily to map their existing development processes and then further struggle to redesign them. But, the true power of value stream mapping lies not in visually depicting the current state of a process, but rather in the actions that are taken and the results achieved by doing so. In other words, the power of the process lies in developing achieved "future states" that provide breakthrough results to an organization. However, if people have difficulty mapping the "current state," they will certainly have difficulty applying "Lean" to it. So, what is the source of this difficulty? How is the development process different from other processes within the organization?

First, development processes are often highly variable and users of value stream mapping often have difficulty depicting such processes. There are several possible root causes for this variability. Understanding these root causes will better allow the user to apply the value stream mapping tool and begin to consider how to address and minimize the root causes in the future state. A partial list of potential causes is provided below, along with various "mapping tips" to be considered when depicting these causes on a current state map.

■ The same development resources are performing multiple tasks within roughly the same period of time. These tasks can include both highly variable knowledge creation activities and less variable knowledge reuse activities as well as various development support activities that are more administrative or transactional in nature. First, the product or service "family" needs to be clearly defined prior to the mapping event. Once this is agreed on, all data collected will be in the context of this particular product or service family, as discussed in chapter 1. This will keep the mapping team focused and help the mapping event proceed more smoothly.

Mapping Tip:

We can make a note on the map that particular resources are "shared" across other families, and record our estimate of the percentage of time that the resources spend on a particular activity. Finally, data for the map can be depicted in ranges, with a note detailing why the data falls into this range. An example of how this information can be noted on a value stream map is provided below.

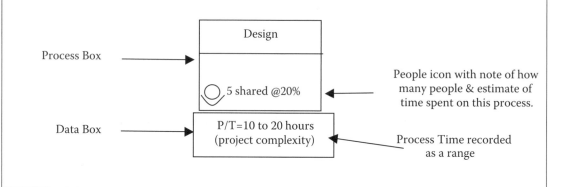

- "Batching" can create variability. In the development process, batching most often refers to the amount of work (in terms of hours) released to the next stage of processing. In the more classic form of batching, design reviews are conducted once a month, design releases completed on Fridays, etc. In such cases, information will remain in a queue until it is periodically processed (i.e., in a "batch").
- Information quality issues can create rework "loops" and, therefore, add more variability in the process. People often struggle with how to depict this on the current state map. There are several ways to depict such loops. What is more important is to understand where they occur and what their impact is on the value stream, rather than trying to depict the numerous paths that the information may take to correct the problem.
- Management may be using development resources to attempt to work on too many design projects simultaneously. This can significantly add to process variability, particularly when problems with one project arise, which can then impact other projects in process at the same time.
- Design personnel are not following standard work practices. Too often, design personnel are left to their own devices to figure out the best way to go about performing various development activities. However, this results in greater process variability. Remember: The means by which the result is achieved is as important as the result itself.
- Insufficient planning is performed, particularly at "shared resource" points (e.g., test labs, production areas). To counter this root cause, the team must understand the manner in which work is prioritized through the value stream.

Mapping Tip:

An important measure of information quality is the percentage of time that all necessary information is received, and whether the information is accurate. This is referred to as "Complete and Accurate." If the information is not Complete and Accurate, the team can record this in a data box, indicating where within the flow the problem was discovered (see example below). If it takes several iterations to finally correct the problem, this can be noted by use of the iteration icon. The impact on the value stream—for example, on lead time—of missing or inaccurate information, along with batching practices, can be recorded as well. The example below indicates what this information might look like on the Value Stream Map:

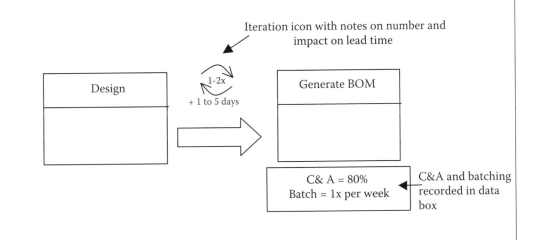

Mapping Tip:

The "in-box" icon can be used to depict the number of development projects currently underway, as well as how this work is prioritized. Expressing data in ranges, with notes explaining what these ranges mean, can highlight the lack of standard work practices. One way to depict this information on the map is shown below.

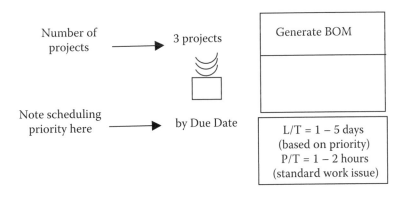

You can begin to see that a large portion of the variability in the development process is created by organizations themselves. Current management practices and the way the company is currently organized to process development-related work could contribute to variability in the process.

The complexity of the existing process is another issue that the Lean practitioner must grapple with, as he or she tackles the development process. Few companies have adequately documented their current development processes. Others have, but not to the degree required by value stream mapping; for example, by identifying all necessary data needed to provide "eyes for flow" and "eyes for waste." Therefore, the creation of the first current state map can be quite frustrating. The complexity of the development process can take several forms. Most commonly, the current development process tends to have many hand-offs over a long period of time. These characteristics scream for the application of Lean and its focus on lead time reduction. Users of the mapping tool, however, can struggle to determine the proper way to depict this information.

Always ask this question: Will we gain any new knowledge by adding detail? For example, people have attempted to put a value stream map in the form of "functional swim lanes." One example had eleven "lanes" on the map—a very deep pool, indeed. When asked why they depicted the information in this way, the team responded that it was "to really highlight the complexity of the current process." Development processes are already very complex. Do we really need to complicate the value stream map to make this point? Would not simple summary measures of the number of departments involved (eleven, in this case) and the number of hand-offs (one hundred seventy-nine) makes the same points?

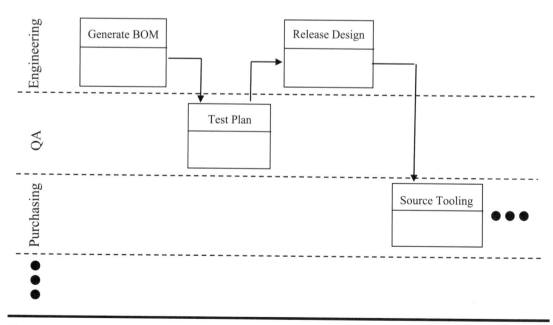

Figure 2.1   An example of swim lane.

Do we need to add "depth" to the map? Process steps that actually happen in parallel should be depicted in parallel. This adds "depth" to the map while accurately depicting *when* things really happen. When Leaning the development process, knowing when things happen tends to be more important than knowing who performs a task. If the group feels that it is important to identify the function or functions that perform a particular process, a simple note in each process box can convey the desired information.

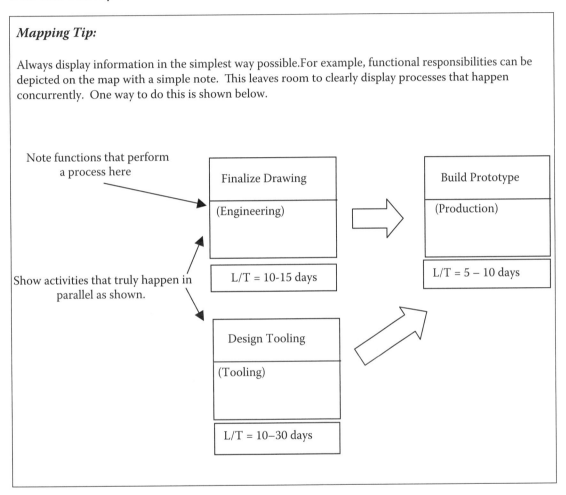

Another factor that can make the development process different is customer and/or industry limitations. There are regulatory requirements that must be met in particular industries. Although these don't typically make the mapping of the current state more difficult, these requirements must be considered when designing the future state. The key here is not to assume. Organizations in regulated industries, for example, often assume that regulators will not accept the changes that they are considering. Such assumptions must be challenged and either verified or disproved. Organizations are sometimes surprised by the positive response that they receive from auditors or regulatory agencies, in general.

Waste in the development process can be difficult to see. However, if we use the value stream mapping tool properly, these wastes will become very apparent. How to identify development waste will be examined in chapter 3.

Chapter 3

Identifying Development Waste

As previously noted, the key to value stream mapping and "Lean" thinking, in general, is to create "eyes for flow" and "eyes for waste." In this chapter, we will review the eight categories of waste and explain how they apply to the development process. The Lean practitioner has keen eyes for waste, seeing specific activities for what they truly are—waste or nonvalue-added—rather than overlooking them, as is so often the case.

Eight Categories of Waste

Taiichi Ono, a former executive at Toyota, identified seven categories of waste. Many in the Lean community consider there to be an eighth category—*Underutilized People*—that can have significant importance to the development process. The eight categories of waste are

- *Overproduction*: In overproduction, organizations produce more information or provide greater service than is needed, sooner than is needed either by the next process step or by the end user or customer. The impetus behind overproduction is the impulse to "stay ahead." Although this reasoning is commendable, it creates other problems and other wastes. For example, information is more subject to change and can even become out-of-date if it is processed too early.
- *Waiting*: Information or services can wait for numerous reasons, thereby impeding flow. To reduce the likelihood of this type of waste, organizations must focus on the necessary information itself or on the customer, not on the people performing the work. People can generally keep busy at all times. However, if a customer has to wait beyond an acceptable time frame, customer satisfaction will decline. If, for whatever reason, information must wait, other problems will arise, such as declines in customer service or a rise in quality-related issues.
- *Transportation*: Transportation refers to the movement of information or a service, either manually or electronically. Although it requires little physical

effort, even the electronic transportation of information can be considered wasteful. The issue with transportation waste is not solely the time required, but the other problems that arise with each transfer. For example, the potential for information to end up in another queue waiting to be processed increases with each transfer, as does the potential to lose information. Quality tends to decline with each transfer of information.

■ *Nonvalue Added (NVA) Processing (or Overprocessing)*: NVA (or overprocessing) occurs when teams expend extra effort beyond what is actually needed by the customer. Extra steps or entire processes within the development process fall into this category, including many of the administrative activities performed in support of the development process. While it may not be possible to eliminate them all, at the very least, the amount of time and effort to perform them can be reduced.

■ *Excess Inventory*: Excess inventory is more than the absolute minimum required to maintain uninterrupted flow of information or service. People will often "batch" development activities. Most often they do so because they believe that it is more efficient. Sometimes there are real reasons to batch development activities, such as system limitations. The root causes for all such practices need to be addressed in order to allow for more flexible processing.

■ *Defects (or Correction)*: This type of waste refers to the discovery and correction of information or a service that has been processed incorrectly or is missing altogether. The correction and clarification of information as it flows through a company can require tremendous effort and cost. To counter this unnecessary expenditure of resources and effort, organizations must address the root causes for the lack of complete and accurate information. Information or service "defects" simply cannot be allowed to continue and become the norm in any company.

■ *Excess Motion*: Although organizations rarely consider this category when looking for ways to trim waste, excess motion by employees in the course of their work can, in fact, be a significant waste category. For example, if employees need to consistently travel to different parts of the building in order to reach necessary supplies, they are likely to be less efficient and less productive than they would be if the supplies were within easy reach.

■ *Underutilized People*: In this instance, staff members are not using their full skills and abilities. People are often given very limited roles and responsibilities when, in reality, they can assume much more if the process has been designed effectively.

Lean Note

The application of all eight wastes to service processes may be a stretch. The nature of many service processes does not typically allow for excess inventory (or batching) or even overproduction. Nonetheless, all of the others most certainly apply.

Although most people are now familiar with these waste terms, they may still have difficulty in recognizing them in the development process, and some have contended that the terms do not apply to the development process at all. Regardless of whether an organization develops a product, a process, or a service, these terms are, in fact, all applicable. Going Lean requires that people expand their existing, sometimes narrow, definitions for these now-common terms.

To assist the Lean practitioner in developing "eyes for waste," Table 3.1 provides select examples for each waste category. It is important to note that the eight wastes are fundamentally interrelated and may overlap; in other words, the examples below may fit into more than one category.

Table 3.1 Development Waste Examples

Overproduction	■ Completing design elements that are not needed for some time ■ Including features that the customer does not see as a value (could also be included in nonvalue-added or overprocessing waste) ■ "Over-engineering"
Waiting	■ Approvals from superiors ■ A lack of available capacity ■ Input from customers ■ System response time ■ Completion of other design elements
Transportation	■ E-mailing information ■ Multiple hand-offs ■ Report distribution ■ Circulating paperwork for signatures
Nonvalue-Added Processing (or Overprocessing)	■ Reentering data ■ Extra copies ■ Unnecessary or excessive reports or paperwork ■ Redesigning something that already has been designed (i.e., reinventing the wheel) ■ Most engineering support services
Excess Inventory	■ Filled in-boxes (electronic or paper) ■ Batch processing transactions ■ "Large" design releases ■ Retaining documents beyond what is required
Defects (or Correction)	■ Design errors ■ Service failures ■ Engineering change orders due to errors ■ Not clearly understanding customer needs ■ Missing or incomplete information
Excess Motion	■ Going to/from printer, fax machine, central filing, and meetings ■ Travel
Underutilized People	■ Limited authority and responsibility for basic tasks ■ Management "command and control" ■ Not sufficiently sharing knowledge ■ Not involving suppliers early in the development process ■ Not involving manufacturing early in the development process

Clearly, this is a partial list; different organizations will produce different examples specific to their own development processes and corporate culture. However, there are key wastes often found in development processes regardless of organizational context. We describe these key wastes next.

Most Common Development Wastes

Defect or correction waste is typically the most glaring waste identified upon review of the current state and the primary focus of the first future state or states. The issue with information quality is apparent in the complete and accurate measures for the specific process steps depicted by using the process and data box icons, which are discussed in more detail in chapter 4 and chapter 5. In addition, we can calculate another measure that summarizes the information quality for the entire value stream. This is called "first pass yield" and is also known as "first time quality" and "roll throughput yield." First pass yield is calculated by multiplying the decimal equivalents for the numerous "complete and accurate" process measures (Table 3.2).

Normally, the first pass yield calculation for development processes is *less than* 40 percent, and often near zero, as incorrect or missing information is allowed to escape from process to process and stage to stage. Why does this occur? Experience tells us that it is usually the result of a lack of awareness of the information needs of subsequent process steps.

The information quality issue can be quickly and effectively addressed with the use of checklists, which are an integral part of nearly all development process future states. Indeed, the use of checklists is widespread throughout the Toyota Product Development System. The difference in Toyota is that there is tremendous discipline in their use, and that they are "living documents" (updated periodically to continuously improve the development process). These checklists should attend to the information needs of all downstream processes, including suppliers, and, in the case of manufacturers, production.

Another prevalent waste within the current state of most development processes is nonvalue-added processing or overprocessing. Often, people involved in the development process—whether they are developing products or services—spend an inordinate amount of time and effort to reinvent the wheel.

Table 3.2

Process	Complete and Accurate
#1	.90 (or 90%)
#2	.80 (or 80%)
#3	.95 (or 95%)
#4	.75 (or 75%)
First Pass Yield	**.51 (or 51%)** (= .9 × .8 × .95 × .75)

Why would developers, engineers, or designers reinvent the wheel? Often, the answer is a lack of awareness of preexisting designs or a reluctance to use them. Less-experienced engineers may be reluctant to ask more senior engineers for guidance regarding designs that can be reused, perhaps for fear that they will be perceived as less capable. Or perhaps more senior engineers are no longer available to give this guidance. If these engineers have moved on, the knowledge that they possess may have been lost forever.

Another possible cause for NVA processing may be that, in the current state, it is *easier* to reinvent the wheel than to identify, locate, and reuse existing designs. A walk-through of the development process often reveals difficulty in finding the necessary information. People involved in the development process struggle to find something similar to use as a starting point, such as a similar product design or a similar proposal for a service, that will fit the need. They perform numerous queries on existing systems until they find something comparable. Existing systems simply are not set up properly to allow for the rapid identification of pertinent information. However, knowledge-based system tools of some form can be very effective in reducing NVA processing waste. Therefore, they are often a part of the first future state or states.

Lean Example

A study at one automotive parts company revealed that approximately 85 percent of all design activities really involved the reuse of preexisting designs. The study also revealed that people in the development process typically spent nearly 50 percent of their day identifying preexisting designs either with "fishing expeditions" through existing engineering systems or by asking more senior engineers for direction. The fishing expeditions consisted of "where used" searches by part numbers of the bill-of-material database, followed by a review of engineering documentation to determine applicability to meet the current need. Multiple iterations of this process were often necessary before the appropriate information was found. In its future state, the company implemented a query tool based on key product characteristics. The time to find a preexisting design that met a need was reduced by 90 percent. The tool took approximately six months to develop, but it saved an estimated 3.5 hours per day, per engineer.

A third key waste found in the current state of most development processes is overproduction, typically in the form of overengineering. Providing features, options, or services that the customer sees no value in is clear waste and can be very costly to a business. Misunderstanding true customer needs can be altogether catastrophic to a business. However, few companies truly take the time necessary to understand customer needs; in other words, to listen to the voice of the customer (VOC). Further, few companies have effective methods to capture and interpret VOC information. In fact, in some design-to-order companies—companies where each order is different and must be designed to some degree—there is a reluctance to ask the customer-probing questions designed to extract this critical information.

Why would some companies be reluctant to collect important VOC information? There are multiple answers to this question. Companies are often concerned with how they might be perceived by their customers or a potential customer (e.g., "Other suppliers don't ask these questions."). The companies may be dealing with a particular customer representative who is not in a position to answer such questions, such as the purchasing person who does not fully understand the requirements for the products or services that he/she seeks to buy.

Still another reason for the reluctance to collect VOC information may be that of time. "We don't have time. By the time we receive the request for a quote or even the order, we're already two weeks behind schedule." Obtaining VOC information early in the development process by effective and efficient means is critical to reducing overproduction waste and is often a part of the first future state or states.

Lean Example

At one design-to-order company in the air handling industry, it was clear that staff was not effectively identifying customer requirements early in the process. This fact was often discovered well into the development process, even as late as the installation process. After overcoming an initial reluctance to do so, the company developed questionnaires that technical sales personnel could use during site visits with potential customers. Rather than viewing this negatively, potential customers saw this as an additional service not offered by other potential suppliers. In fact, the company developed several important partnering relationships that helped them to increase their business. Further, the additional lead time up front (on average one additional week) translated to a lead-time reduction of three weeks on the "back end," and a net lead-time reduction in the overall process of two weeks. Equally important, field service costs were reduced by approximately 50 percent, as there were fewer corrections during installation.

Waiting is another major waste most often seen in the current state of most development processes. Typically, the difference between overall lead time and total process time is, by definition, waste. A major contributor to the difference between the lead time and total process time is often waiting waste. Development projects wait to be worked on for various reasons: the availability of resources, approvals, and additional information, to name just a few. The typical sequential nature of a development process may also be a contributor, as waiting tends to increase with the number of process steps and hand-offs.

> **Lean Note**
>
> Comparing overall lead time to total process time may not be appropriate for development processes that already involve a lot of concurrent activities. This is particularly true for large development projects that require thousands of hours to complete over one to two years, as seen in large aerospace or military applications. However, for most other development processes, it is a good indication of waste.

Simple opportunities to reduce waiting waste are usually identified in the first future state or states. As previously stated, the wastes tend to be interrelated. Waiting waste can usually be reduced by improving information quality as well as by removing NVA processing and freeing up capacity, which was described earlier. Still another opportunity may be to streamline approval processes, and reduce hand-offs in general.

> **Lean Example**
>
> At one aerospace company, the eleven signatures required on every engineering document were reduced to four. Seven people admitted to adding no value to the process and were simply "rubber stamping" the documents, deferring to the judgment of others who had already signed them. The result was a twenty-one-day decrease in lead time for approvals.

The discussion in this chapter is intended to prompt the Lean practitioner to look at work in a different way. Perhaps he or she will see particular activities, often some that have become a standard part of the process, for what they truly represent—activities that create no value for the customer and that must be challenged, streamlined, and eliminated if possible. In chapter 4, we will build on the content covered in this and prior chapters, to develop an effective current state map.

> **Lean Note**
>
> Performing a waste identification exercise as part of the mapping team's training prior to creating the current state map can be both beneficial and fun. Team members will select several waste categories and identify as many specific examples as they can for each from their own development process. It is a type of brainstorming exercise, so team members must guard against trying to resolve particular ones and just continue to identify examples. For large groups, consider breaking up the participants into smaller groups and assigning particular waste categories to each. Have each group "report out" to the other. Typically, thirty to forty-five minutes is spent on the exercise. The exercise can be used to help the team members develop "eyes for waste."

Chapter 4

Assessing the Current State

The creation of a development process's current state map will be much easier if the reader has properly prepared for the mapping event that was described in chapter 1. To recall, the preparation step culminated with the creation of the SIPOC (supplier–input–process–output–customer)-scoping document, which succinctly summarized various aspects of the mapping effort. With this document in hand, the identified mapping team will be better equipped to assess the current state.

The current state map is a visual depiction of how the existing process works. Although individual team members and the organization overall will understand portions of the existing development process, few people will have a solid understanding of how the entire process really works. Further, there likely has been little or no attempt in the past to truly measure the effectiveness and efficiency of the existing process in terms of cost, service, and quality. As we will see in this chapter, the inclusion of specific, relevant data on the map is what makes value stream mapping a powerful assessment tool, and distinguishes it from traditional process mapping. There are six suggested steps for completing a current state map. These six steps are outlined below.

Suggested Steps to Complete a Current State Map

1. Identify current customer needs.
2. Identify main processes (in order).
3. Select process metrics (or data attributes).
4. Perform value stream walk-through and fill in data boxes.
5. Establish how each process prioritizes work.
6. Calculate value stream summary metrics such as lead time, process time, first pass yield, cost, and other measures that the mapping team deems important.

Step 1: Identify Current Customer Needs

In this step, we are referring to the external customer; the end user of the product or service that is being developed. Various aspects of customer needs should be considered. First, what is the lead time (the time to market for new products or services) currently requested by customers? Be clear on the definition of lead time with regard to the starting and ending points. What is the current rate of demand on the development process? This could be measured in several ways, such as number of projects per year, number of models or styles per year, number of orders per month (for design-to-order companies), etc. To display the variability in demand, organizations are encouraged to express the demand in a range. How will we express the performance of the current process in meeting customer expectations? In other words, what measure of quality performance will be used? There are several to choose from, including, but not limited to, warranty costs, complaints, customer satisfaction ratings, returns. Most often several quality-related measures are included on the current state map and can be displayed as shown in Figure 4.1.

Step 2: Identify Main Processes (In Order)

The key processes will be identified and recorded in the process boxes in the order in which they take place. First, we need to make a decision regarding the level of detail desired. In other words, how many process boxes should we have? When should one process box end and the next one begin? There are several guidelines to consider, the most important of which is time, specifically, lead time.

   To recall, we use value stream mapping to create "eyes for flow" and "eyes for waste." We want to identify points in the value stream where flow stops and queue begins. However, we do not want to highlight every stoppage of flow, just the significant ones. What makes one stoppage significant and another not? The answer comes from comparing the typical length of time of the stoppage to the overall lead time for the development process. If the overall lead time is two hundred days, we certainly should not concern ourselves with stoppages of minutes or hours. If there is a queue in between two process steps and it is deemed insignificant, then we should consider combining the boxes, as shown in Figure 4.2.

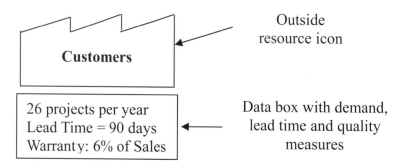

Figure 4.1   Displaying Customer Needs.

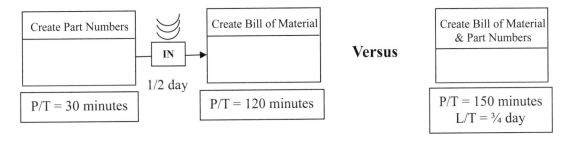

Figure 4.2 Two process boxes versus one.

The same discussion can take place with "process time," the time that it takes to perform particular processes. If the current process involves 400 people hours, we probably should not concern ourselves with processes that require several minutes to complete. We may want to consider combining quickly performed processes with other boxes, along with appropriate notes, to avoid confusion.

Another consideration to use when determining the appropriate level of detail is the manner in which to address the numerous development support processes. The pitfall to watch for during this part of the mapping process is that the team may begin to lose sight of the development process itself and become overwhelmed by the various processes performed to support the development process. Although we do not want to overlook these processes and their part in the development value steam, we certainly do not want to get into too much detail for each.

Figure 4.2 provides a good example of how the processes can be handled. In a product development process that requires the creation of part numbers and bills of materials, it may be out of scope to redesign these elements of the development system. However, it is still important to see how these necessary processes fit in the current system. Combining two (or more) process steps into a single process box with an appropriate data box beneath it is one way to show the linkages with important support processes, but without overly complicating the current state map.

> ### *Mapping Tip*
>
> Always consider the total lead time and total process time for the current development process when determining the appropriate level of detail for the current state map. Focus on the processes that are significant contributors to both. Excessive detail does not necessarily provide important new knowledge when assessing the current state. Too much detail can really sidetrack a team from the agreed-upon scope of the mapping event.

It is very important to clearly note *when* particular processes are completed in the value stream. Most development processes have some amount of concurrency to them, such as particular processes that are performed in parallel with others. It is important to clearly depict these on the map.

Step 3: Select Process Metrics

Selecting appropriate process metrics for a development process can be troublesome because most development processes have no standard performance metrics reflecting cost, service, and quality within the value stream. Many data attributes used in production or office mapping can be useful in a development map if we broaden their definitions. In addition, there are distinct metrics and particular processes that lend themselves well to the development value stream.

It is important to understand how the data will be used to analyze the current state and in designing a future state. Certainly, we want to highlight waste. The discussion in chapter 3 on "identifying development waste" should help us to select process metrics that will do just that. But, there is more to consider. We also will need to understand how this data will be obtained from the existing development process. While it is ideal to obtain this data through firsthand observation, this may not always be possible. Perhaps this data can be obtained from historic records or even through people's best guess. At the higher level, or "balcony" view (i.e., less detail), which value stream mapping usually represents, best guess estimates usually work just fine.

Mapping Tip

The data collection process should have been discussed during the preparation step, which occurs prior to the mapping event. Perhaps important historic data could have been pulled together ahead of time. During the actual walk-through of the current state, approximately 20 minutes will be spent discussing each process box. This should be taken into consideration when determining how best to collect the process data during the mapping event.

Next, we will explore several possible development process data attributes and will discuss how they might be used to assess the current state or in the development of the future state. Development process data attributes include:

- Process time (including ranges)
- Available time
- Number of people involved
- Lead time or turnaround time (including wait time)
- Number of iterations
- Typical batch size or frequency a task is performed
- Percent complete and accurate (a measure of information quality)
- Rework or revisions (such as design changes)
- Inventory or queues of information
- Demand rate
- Information technology used or sources of information

The above list can be quite overwhelming at first glance. However, several of the data attributes overlap; they express the same information, just in different ways. It is a good idea to express the data in the form of a range and to add a note detailing the cause of the variability or project complexity.

Process Time, Available Time, and Number of People

Process time, otherwise known as "touch time," refers to the actual time required to complete a task, and is a measure of work content. It can usually be obtained through observation of the process, or it can be estimated by staff members. For example, it takes fifty minutes to enter a bill-of-material (BOM) from beginning to end, uninterrupted. Process times may vary for various reasons (individual capability, size of the BOM). When this happens, the team should discuss whether the variation represents different service families, or if some other explanation exists.

It is important to understand work content at various points of the development value stream. The mapping team can focus on those points that demonstrate the most work content to identify waste reduction and other streamlining opportunities. Work content is also examined in conjunction with the number of people assigned to the development process and an estimate of "available time" to determine current capacity at various points of the value stream.

Available time is the percentage of time that the required resources—both staffing and equipment—are actually available to perform a process. This number is often obtained by asking people, "What percentage of your time do you spend on this task?" Most resources involved in the development process perform multiple tasks. It is important to understand how they spend their time. They may not be as available to perform a particular task as often as management may believe. By comparing capacity to demand rate, bottlenecks or constraints in the current system can be identified. The manner in which process time, available time, and number of people can be depicted on the current state map is shown in Figure 4.3.

Lead Time

Lead time is the elapsed time associated with completing an activity, from the time it enters the inbox to the time the completed activity leaves the responsible

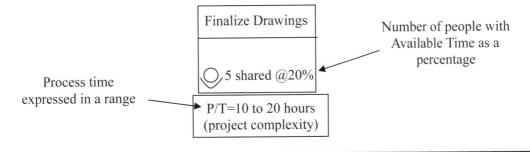

Figure 4.3 Depicting process time, number of people, and available time.

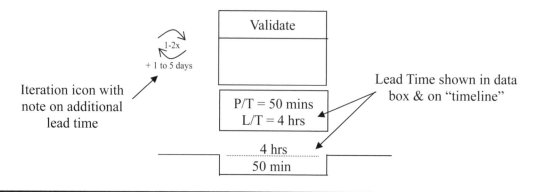

Figure 4.4   Depicting lead time and iterations.

employee's desk. If a staff member leaves an activity incomplete, only to finish it at a later point, lead time increases beyond process time. For example, it may take just fifty minutes to validate a design (i.e., process time). However, questions might arise and the validation process may then be put aside for a period of time. Therefore, the fifty-minute validation task may actually take four hours to complete (i.e., lead time) while the work is in the queue awaiting answers. Reasons for excessive lead time (e.g., multiple interruptions) can be depicted in the mapping process, as shown in Figure 4.4.

Number of Iterations

This can be an important data attribute due to the iterative nature of development processes. The information can be noted in a data box or by use of the iteration icon. Very importantly, the impact on lead time and/or process time should be noted as well. The manner in which this can be depicted on the current state map is shown in Figure 4.4.

Typical Batch Size or Frequency

This data attribute can be related to lead time and is often used in its place. For example, if a task is performed once each week, the lead time will be one week. In other words, the information can remain in queue for up to one week before it is processed. However, batching in a design process can take other forms. In general, it represents the *amount* of work being released to the next process. For example, BOMs are released to the production system once a week. This would represent a batch size of one week. Another batch size example might be the release of large design elements rather than smaller elements. Batching has a big impact on flow, as downstream processes wait for necessary information. Future state designs often consider the impact of the release of smaller design elements on the flow of the overall development process.

> ### *Lean Example*
>
> A company in the defense industry had been implementing Lean in its manu-facturing operations for several years. As process and lead time were reduced in production, operations waited more and more for information from design engineering. One of the root causes for this waiting waste was that the pro-duct was designed (and built) in one hundred fifty main modules. Each module could represent thousands of hours of work. The company decided to design the product in three hundred modules (i.e., reduce the batch size of design), and reap the benefits of reduced lead time by doing so.

Percent Complete and Accurate, Rework and Revisions

This is a general process quality metric used to describe how often complete and accurate information is received at a particular process step by the person or persons performing that step. It is usually noted on the map from the perspec-tive of the recipient. Paperwork or other transactions might not contain necessary information or may contain inaccurate information. This is a very important mea-sure in development processes. It clearly highlights defect or correction waste. However, there may be other quality-related metrics that can be obtained and included in the current state map; percentage of test failures or number of engi-neering change notices are just two examples.

This data may be obtained through historic records or, once again, through estimates provided by the people performing the work. It is common to ask the people performing the work to identify the most frequent problems that they encounter; for example, to tell the team the top three problems with regard to frequency or impact. These can be noted and attached to the current state map, if desired. The mapping team will need to acquire examples of these problems so that they can better understand the issues.

Inventory or Queues

Inventory can take many forms in development processes and represents queues of information—symptoms of a lack of flow. Inventory typically resides as paper-work or electronic files. The unit of measure can vary based on the nature of the process step within the development system. Examples include:

■ Various forms in people's in-boxes
■ Design projects in queue or underway
■ Line items awaiting Purchasing to process, etc.

Look for piles of paperwork or electronic queues of information. Inventory is normally associated with batch processing and long lead time. Queues can be clearly noted using the inbox icon as shown in Figure 4.5.

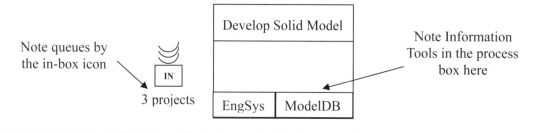

Figure 4.5   Depicting queues and information technology.

Demand Rate

Demand represents the volume of transactions seen at each process over a specified period of time, such as orders per day, projects per week, etc. The range of demand should also be noted, if applicable, along with a note explaining the variation. For example, at one company, 80 percent of the BOMs were completed in the last week of each month. As previously mentioned, this type of information can be used to compare to current capacity to identify bottlenecks or constraints in the development value stream.

Information Technology Used

"Information technology used" describes the tools used to assist the processing of the information at each process box or the sources of information that are needed to perform a process. Most often it refers to software tools, databases, and the like. These tools are recorded in a lower corner of the process box (see Figure 4.5). There may be several technologies used within a process box, and several others used in different process boxes. This apparent lack of integration can be a root cause for long lead times, lack of flow, extra processing, and quality-related problems. To accurately map these issues, the mapping team might ask the staff performing the work to identify particular information tools that they rely on and to demonstrate their use. The manner in which this can be depicted on the current state map is shown in Figure 4.5.

Only data that will be used to effectively assess the current state or will be used to develop the future state should be included in the process metrics. If no purpose is foreseen, then the data should not be obtained and included on the map. Some of the data will be recorded in the data box icon below the process box, while other data will be noted adjacent to the appropriate mapping icon.

Step 4: Perform Value Stream Walk-Through and Fill in Data Boxes

Going to the *gemba* (Japanese for "actual place" or where work is performed) and walking the flow is critical to a successful value stream mapping event. People spend far too much time in conference or meeting rooms when mapping and much important information is lost as a result. This is true for numerous reasons. First, although team members may believe that they understand what is being explained to them by others, they, in fact, may be missing the point altogether. Without observing the work being performed at the same time as a team, there is a great opportunity for failure in the important communication process that takes place during the mapping event.

Further, when value stream maps are created solely in conference or meeting rooms, the nature of the work environment will not be apparent. Mapping team members will not observe the numerous interruptions and disruptions that can occur, the distance between resources, obstacles to communication and teamwork, and other issues associated with the work environment.

A third point to make is that people will often overlook important aspects of the process when describing them to others in a meeting room, such as reference materials kept at a person's desk or other important sources of information. Only at the *gemba* will the team really understand how the work is processed.

> ### *Lean Note*
>
> As noted above, the term *gemba* means "actual place" in Japanese, and is often used to refer to any place where value-creating work occurs. Discussing problems or improvement opportunities away from where the actual work is performed can lend itself to mistakes; mistakes in understanding the problem and in the decisions to correct them. "Going to the *gemba*" can overcome the most basic pitfalls in communication and problem solving. "Going to the *gemba*" is a practice that all Lean thinkers must follow. It is at the *gemba* that the answers exist.

Now, it is not always possible to physically observe all development work that is performed. Some development processes span years and hundreds, even thousands, of hours. Nevertheless, a walk-through can still be possible, though actual observation is not. In such cases, estimates of process time are provided by the people performing the work, or through historic records. Important information can still be gathered, such as the nature of the work environment, demonstration of the information technology tools that are used, and examples of information quality issues that affect the current state.

Another obstacle to walking the flow involves the physical location of the various development resources. Are they located within the same building? Are they in different buildings in the same complex? Are they located in different geographic regions? Answers to these questions will determine if more time is needed for the mapping event, where the mapping event should take place (i.e., where the majority of the work is performed), and how offsite activities will be handled.

Perhaps a "virtual tour" can occur for processes performed offsite. Particular team members can have access to the information technology tools that they use, can bring examples of documents and problems with them, and can walk the team through their part of the process virtually. Although this is not ideal, it may be the best that can be done during the mapping event. Perhaps a physical walk-through of the other site can be scheduled at a later time, particularly if the assessment of the current state dictates such an event. Generally speaking, the team will spend approximately twenty minutes onsite per process box. One mapping team member can be identified as a timekeeper, keeping the team to the twenty-minute limit and moving things along.

Step 5: Establish How Each Process Prioritizes Work

During the walk-through, the mapping team should ask the people performing the work a simple question, such as, "How do you prioritize your work?" or "How do you know what to do next?" The responses are often interesting. The answers may also differ along the value stream. In other words, people may be working to different priorities. Remember that many resources in the development process perform multiple tasks, and can even work on multiple projects at any time. Therefore, the opportunity for schedule conflicts increases. Scheduling priorities on the current state map is usually noted adjacent to the inbox icon. This is shown in Figure 4.6.

Step 6: Calculate Value Stream Summary Metrics

On their return from the walk-through, the team will summarize the performance of the current development system. There are several value stream summary measures to choose from. The most commonly used ones are total lead time, total process time, first pass yield, and total cost. To estimate cost, the team should consider using the process time information, as well as materials, and costs associated with quality issues, such as failures, warranties, etc. Other summary measures that a team should consider are number of hand-offs and number of people or departments involved. As with the process data, the value stream summary metrics can also take the form of a range. For example, consider several expressions of lead time (e.g., successful projects versus not-so-successful projects, concept to release to production versus concept to shipment of first production units).

In the next chapter, we will apply what has been covered in the first four chapters to create a current state map for our case study, DevelopTek.

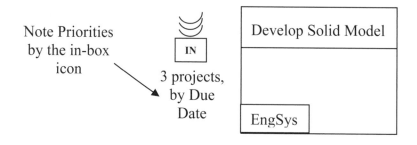

Figure 4.6   Displaying scheduling priorities.

Mapping Tips

- Keep the size of the mapping team to six to ten people. There is a tendency for people to disengage and even wander off in larger groups. While it may be commendable to want to get more people involved, involvement can take various forms. For example, the mapping team can visit the work areas of people not on the mapping team. The people performing the work will describe their activities to the mapping team. This is a form of involvement.

- Be sure that team members stay focused and engaged. The mapping event is usually the first opportunity for many people to really learn how things work overall. Team members should be very interested in doing so. However, it is easy for people to become distracted and "pulled away" from the mapping effort during the walk-through. Team members must resist this throughout the mapping event.

- Assign responsibilities to team members. One person can be the timekeeper and another can be an interviewer who will ask people questions to collect the data agreed on for each process box. Some members can actually demonstrate the work being performed. Still other members can be asked to retrieve particular data and information.

- Have the person performing the work demonstrate the process, providing a narration while doing so. Have team members hold their questions until after the demonstration has been completed. If time allows, have the person demonstrate the process again.

- The twenty minutes per process rule is a guideline. Some process boxes can be reviewed in less time, others will require more. Consider the time allotted for developing the current state map and the number of process boxes identified. Perhaps more or less time will be necessary so that the mapping event will end on time. The timekeeper can point out to the team that the twenty minutes have elapsed and ask whether they want to spend more time on the process.

- Be flexible; there is no single correct current state map. There is more than one way to depict the data and information collected. Just remember to keep it simple.

- Ask questions and have a scribe make notes on important points that have been brought up for future reference. A great practice is to ask "why" several times. It is a practice that leads people to more meaningful responses.

- Map the entire value stream as a team. Avoid having different people mapping different segments of the value stream. Remember, team members will come into the mapping event understanding portions of the value stream. The goal is that, upon creating the current state map, they will have an understanding of the overall system.

Chapter 5

Developing a Current State Map for DevelopTek

In this chapter, we will apply the six-step process to complete a current state map for DevelopTek, a fictitious company. First, we will introduce the company and provide some background information. DevelopTek designs and manufactures components for specific workplace or facility applications. Currently, a typical project requires approximately six months to release and to verify a new design into production. However, Sales, under pressure from the market, is requesting a much quicker turnaround: approximately three months. Engineering and Manufacturing have struggled to cut their lead time by the necessary 50 percent. Further, the reputation of the company is suffering as a result of trying to speed up the process, only to find problems upon installation at the customer location. Potential repeat business and new orders have been lost as a result. Warranty costs are now 6 percent of sales revenue for new products.

DevelopTek's development process involves the following steps:

- Define requirements
- Develop initial specifications
- Design prototype
- Redesign
- Build prototype
- Test Prototype
- Create final drawings and bill of materials (BOMs)
- Source tooling
- Develop process documentation
- Release to production
- Verify the design

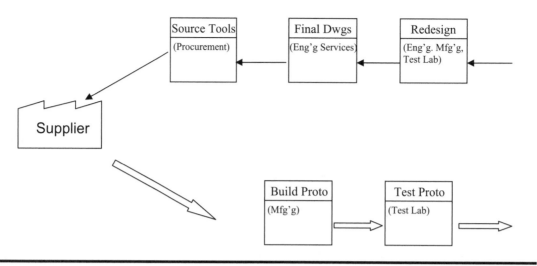

Figure 5.1   Current state map identifying 11 main processes.

The following functions or departments are involved in the process: Sales, Engineering, Engineering Services, Manufacturing, the Test Lab, Procurement, and Manufacturing Engineering.

Historically, the company has processed approximately twenty-six projects per year. Launch schedules with due dates are created for each project, but these dates are rarely met. The company must consider significant changes in its traditional approach to designing new products if it is to remain competitive and meet market needs.

We will use the value stream mapping icons and the various mapping tips outlined in chapter 1 through chapter 4 to develop a current state map for DevelopTek. DevelopTek's current state map is illustrated in Figure 5.1A/B. (The figures are to be read side by side.)

Developmental Processes of DevelopTek

Step 1: Identifying Current Customer Needs

The current state mapping process always begins with identifying current customer needs and other customer-related information. At this point, we usually consider external customers because internal customers should be included within the development value stream. Performing this step first is important because it helps the team begin to see the development process from the perspective of the customer. We use the rectangle information icon to show that requirements-related information (Reqs) is provided by the customer to DevelopTek.

Step 2: Identifying Main Processes (In Order)

There are eleven main processes defined for the DevelopTek case study as noted previously. The functions or departments that are involved in each of these

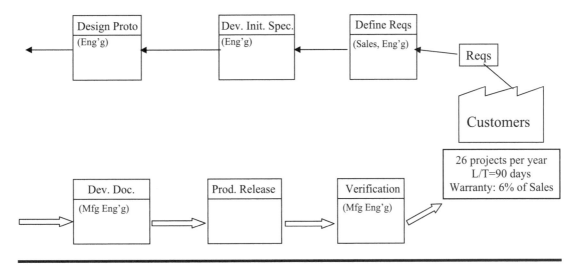

Figure 5.1 (*Continued*)

processes are noted within the appropriate process box. Finally, the outside resource icon is used to depict the suppliers. As we will see, the process involves both tooling and material suppliers. A data box for the suppliers will be provided later in the chapter.

Mapping Tip

For this case study, we will use a "closed loop" format to depict the value stream. This is *not* the only format that can be used to display the information provided. Another format is to simply lay out the process boxes from left to right. Whatever format is used, special care must be given to note tasks that occur in parallel. This is particularly important when summarizing the overall lead time. For this case study, most of the processes occur sequentially, except for the "documentation development" process, which occurs parallel to the supplier lead time for production tooling and materials.

Step 3 and Step 4: Selecting Process Metrics and Filling in Data Boxes

The team identified the key metrics that it wanted to collect and display for each process box. These are provided next for each process box, along with some additional background information for each. It should be noted that all lead times are shown in business days (five days per week) throughout.

Define Requirements

There are two functions or departments involved in this step: Sales and Engineering, and Sales works with Engineering to complete this important task.

Sales may contact the customer numerous times to get more information or clarification of information already provided.

- Process Time (P/T) = 3 people, 8 hours each = 24 hour
- Lead Time (L/T) = 10 days
- Complete and Accurate (C&A) = 80 percent

Develop Initial Specifications

Engineering then works to develop initial specifications. Approximately 50 percent of the time, additional information is needed from Sales and/or the customer in order to develop the specification.

- Process Time (P/T) = 1 person, 40 hours
- Lead Time (L/T) = 5 days awaiting assignment, 10 days to complete work
- Complete and Accurate (C&A) = 50 percent

Design Prototype

Using a computer-based system (ACAD), Engineering then designs a prototype that will be built to prove out the design concepts. Approximately 20 percent of the time, the engineers at this stage discover missing or unclear information as they begin to work out details of the design.

- Process Time (P/T) = 1 person, 80 hours
- Lead Time (L/T) = 20 days
- Complete and Accurate (C&A) = 80 percent

Build Prototype

Manufacturing must then schedule in the building of the prototype with regular production, and create a prototype to prove out the design concepts. Manufacturing will use available materials for the prototype. Approximately 75 percent of the time, Manufacturing can build the prototype without issues arising. In other words, 25 percent of the time, Manufacturing needs to go back to Engineering to correct problems or to obtain clarification of the design.

- Process Time (P/T) = 2 people, 20 hours each = 40 hours
- Lead Time (L/T) = 10 days awaiting start, 5 days to build
- Complete and Accurate (C&A) = 75 percent

Test Prototype

The prototype must then be tested. The Test Lab will schedule in the prototype testing along with its other demands. Approximately 50 percent of the time, the prototype fails the test. In this instance, one to two design iterations will be necessary before an acceptable prototype passes testing.

- Process Time (P/T) = 1 person, 16 hours
- Lead Time (L/T) = 5 days in test queue, 2 days to test
- Percent Pass = 50 percent

Redesign

Based on the test results and in conjunction with Manufacturing and the Test Lab, Engineering will redesign the product. Frequently, the design will pass testing in two or fewer redesign iterations. This process requires additional redesign effort and increases lead time, the amount of which will vary based on the test results.

- Number of Iterations = 0 to 2
- Process Time (P/T) = 1 FTE, 0 to 100 hours
- Lead Time (L/T) = 0 to 30 days
- Complete and Accurate (C&A) = 100 percent

Create Final Drawings and BOMs

Once the prototype passes testing, the design is *finalized*. This falls to the Engineering Services Department to accomplish. Final drawings and bills of material are generated in the Enterprise Resource Planning System (ERP system). The design is then "frozen." Approximately 10 percent of the time, questions regarding the information arise during this step, which must be answered by Engineering.

- Process Time (P/T) = 2 people, 40 hours each = 80 hours
- Lead Time (L/T) = 20 days
- Complete and Accurate (C&A) = 90 percent

Source Tooling

Upon finalizing the design, the Procurement Department is triggered to identify sources for production tooling and materials. Although the company has long-standing relationships with various suppliers, it is still the practice to request quotes from numerous suppliers. It takes about five days for Procurement to get around to processing the necessary request for quotes.

- Process Time (P/T) = 1 person, 16 hours
- Lead Time (L/T) = 5 days in queue

Develop Process Documentation

While the company waits to receive the production tooling and materials, the Manufacturing Engineering Department works to develop the necessary process documentation. The manufacturing engineers use a computer-based tool called DocWrite to accomplish this task.

- Process Time (P/T) = 2 people, 40 hours each = 80 hours
- Lead Time (L/T) = 20 days (while waiting for tooling and materials)
- Complete and Accurate (C&A) = 100 percent

Release to Production

Once all tooling and documentation is available, a formal production release process is completed. Various people from within the organization meet for several hours to review the production documentation and sign off on it. They rarely find any problems during this review process.

- Process Time (P/T) = 4 people, 4 hours each = 16 hours
- Lead Time (L/T) = 5 days to schedule meeting, 1 day to conduct meeting
- Pass/Approval Rate = 100 percent

Verification

In the production phase, the Manufacturing Engineering Department conducts a verification process as the initial production units are completed.

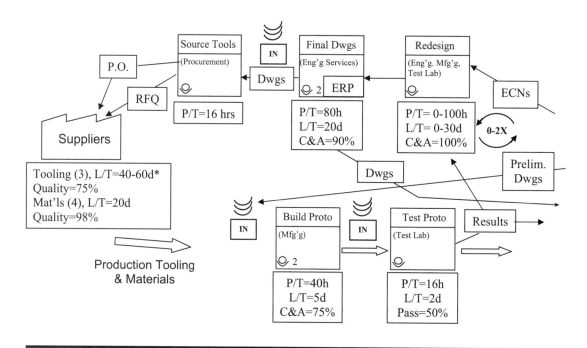

Figure 5.2   Adding data boxes to the current state map.

Any design-related problems found at this time will be addressed with an engineering change notice (ECN). Several problems can be found over time.

- Process Time (P/T) = 1 person, 40 hours
- Lead Time (L/T) = 5 days
- Average Number of ECNs per project: 4

Supplier Data

In this step, the team examines supplier data, or data regarding the tooling and materials used in production for new products. This information is usually provided by Purchasing personnel or perhaps, the suppliers themselves, if they are involved in the mapping event. Included is quality performance information. For example, there is a problem with 25 percent of the tooling received from suppliers for new products. The most frequent cause for this is unclear requirements in the engineering documentation.

Tooling:	Materials:
■ Number of Suppliers = 3	■ Number of Suppliers = 4
■ Lead Time (L/T) = 40 to 60 days	■ Lead Time (L/T) = 20 days
■ Quality Performance = 75 percent	■ Quality Performance = 99 percent

Now let's add the data for each process, as well as supplier data, to the current state map (Figure 5.2A/B). A data box is added for each individual process box. Where appropriate, the people icon will be used within the process

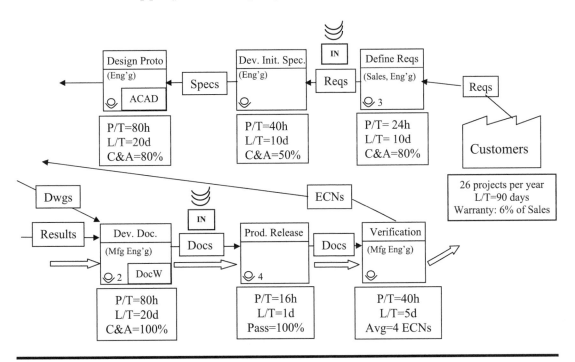

Figure 5.2   (Continued)

box to depict the number of people involved in each process. The Information Technology tools used, when provided, also are noted within the process box.

The points in the value stream in which significant queues can form are highlighted using the inbox icon. Very importantly, the specific information that is created and passed on from process to process is depicted on the current state map using the rectangular information icon. The abbreviations used throughout this example make the map less busy.

Step 5: Establish How Each Process Prioritizes Work

In this example, "launch schedules" were created for each development project. There are due dates for each project. Therefore, employees will prioritize work, based on these due dates, throughout the development process. This is depicted on the current state map in Figure 5.3A/B with a simple note. Once the data have been added to the map, the team can now develop the value stream summary measures.

Step 6: Calculating Value Stream Summary Metrics

The team members calculated an overall lead time for the process. They chose to display this information in a range to emphasize the variability in the current

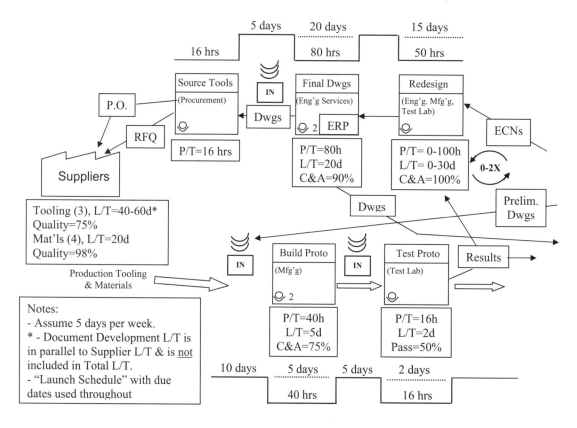

Figure 5.3   Adding value stream summary metrics, including timeline.

process, along with a separate lead time when redesign is required. Special care had to be given to the means by which the processes that occur in parallel (i.e., waiting on supplier lead time, developing documentation) will be handled. The development of process documentation takes twenty days, while the tooling lead time requires forty to sixty days. Given that the tooling lead time is greater, it, therefore, is used for calculating the overall lead time. A note to clarify this is added to the map.

The total process time is calculated simply by adding all of the data for each process box. A separate total process time is calculated when redesign is required. Both the process time and the lead time are shown on a timeline for the top part of the map and another timeline for the bottom part of the map. The timeline helps to highlight the major contributors to lead time and process time. It can also clarify whether the lead time is associated with waiting in queues or occurs within individual processes. Finally, the team calculated a first pass yield (FPY) for the value stream by multiplying the various quality metrics provided for each process (e.g., C&A, Pass). It is estimated to be 8.0 percent. This calculation is illustrated in Table 5.1.

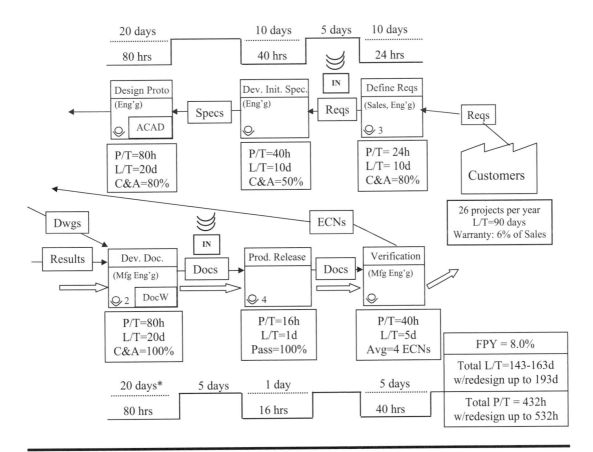

Figure 5.3 *(Continued)*

Table 5.1 First Pass Yield (FPY) Calculation

Process	Quality Measure
Define requirements	.80 (80%)
Develop initial specifications	.50 (50%)
Design prototype	.80 (80%)
Build prototype	.75 (75%)
Test prototype	.50 (50%)
Finalize drawings	.90 (90%)
Develop documentation	1.00 (100%)
Tooling quality	.75 (75%)
Material quality	.99 (99%)
Production release	1.00 (100%)
First Pass Yield	8.0%

> ### *Mapping Tip*
>
> The mapping team should always do a reality check with regard to the value stream summary measures. If the measures do not seem in line with historic performance, then the means to calculate them, as well as any data for particular processes, should be rechecked. At times, the numbers may need a bit of "tightening up." Perhaps the ranges provided were too great. Typically the summary measures can quickly be adjusted to everyone's satisfaction. Remember, there does not need to be precision in the figures, but they do need to be somewhat accurate.

This completes the current state map for the DevelopTek case study. Next, the team reviews the current state and notes their observations or reflections. Reflecting on the current state map is an important step to complete *before* moving on to the future state development. To help prompt the discussion during this reflection step, consider the following questions:

- What wastes do you see?
- What issues of flow are evident?
- Where do queues form? What are some potential root causes for them?
- Are there any issues with regard to how work is prioritized?
- Are any bottlenecks or constraints evident through the value stream?
- How does the overall system performance compare to customer needs?
- What does the system do well?
- Can you identify some "lean" opportunities?

At this point, the team is ready to begin to develop the future state. But, before doing that, the next chapter will review general Lean development principles and compare and contrast them to traditional approaches.

Chapter 6

Lean Development Principles

There are several key concepts upon which every Lean development system is based. In addition, there are specific principles that must be part of every Lean development process. We will start off by discussing the general concepts. A Lean development system is based on:

1. Distinguishing between knowledge reuse and knowledge creation
2. Performing development activities concurrently wherever possible
3. Distinguishing between "good" iterations and "bad" iterations
4. Maintaining a process focus throughout

We will now explore each of these principles and compare and contrast them to the characteristics most often found in traditional development processes.

Distinguishing between Knowledge Reuse and Knowledge Creation

Traditional development processes tend to be very task or transaction oriented. The focus is on completing a task, for example, completing and testing a prototype—or a transaction—such as entering the bills of materials (BOMs) into the system. The result is that, as illustrated in chapter 3, design personnel typically spend as much as 85 percent of their available time on transactional activities rather than on activities that create new knowledge, such as identifying new customer needs and experimentation. We provided an example of this in chapter 3.

In a Lean Enterprise, we generally want to reduce the number and complexity of transactions. This is true in the development process as well. To do this, most organizations must first recognize that most of their design activities involve the reuse of knowledge rather than the creation of new knowledge. Once this hurdle is overcome, organizations can and must develop a highly effective and efficient process for reusing knowledge, and provide that information to the people involved in the design process.

Such systems, in which knowledge can be easily retrieved with minimum effort, have often been referred to as design "libraries." They require organizations to take the time to properly record the knowledge obtained during the development process, and to record it in a form that is easily retrievable. For example, often engineers must remember "like" part numbers or ask more experienced engineers to guide them in the search for "similar" parts. In this way, an engineer can find a "starting point" to streamline the design process. However, this is often a time-consuming process that relies on people's memories. Instead, development personnel should be able to query a database on meaningful performance characteristics in order to find "like" or "similar" parts.

In addition, designers should be encouraged to make use of existing parts or components without altering them unless it is absolutely necessary. Behaviorally, this can represent a big shift from practices in traditional design organizations. People in the development process are often recognized for "creative solutions" that are actually not that creative at all, but rather variations of existing design elements. Further, the variations often do little to better meet customer needs or lower the cost of meeting those needs. Most often they simply result in *increasing* the cost of development.

Lean Example

One automotive manufacturer had several hundred different designs for locking a car door across all of its models, all developed within the past twenty years. The leader in the industry has fewer than twenty. Certainly, the numerous variations of locking mechanisms increase development cost.

Once an effective and efficient process has been developed and provided to design personnel, the time required to reuse knowledge can be significantly reduced. This allows more time for design personnel to engage in true knowledge creation activities (i.e., add value)—a move from "reinventing the wheel" to discovering true innovations in wheel technology. To do so, we need to create knowledge and learn more efficiently without undermining the effectiveness of learning. In other words, we want to employ "rapid learning cycles."

Lean Note

To increase the efficiency of knowledge creation, consider the following tools from the Lean development toolbox.

■ *Trystorming*: In trystorming, the idea is to quickly bring a design concept to a tangible form, so that it can be tried out. People learn more by doing and from practical experience than by other methods. Although the terminology differs, similar methods are used throughout the Toyota Product Development System. The key is to make "fuzzy" as tangible as possible, as quickly as possible, to result in faster and more effective learning cycles.

- *Rapid product prototyping*: Prototypes are quickly developed to improve the learning process. This technique can support the trystorming effort described above.
- *Concurrent or simultaneous engineering*: This technique involves "downstream" participants, such as manufacturing or the supplier, earlier in the learning process. As a result, more thoughtful questions, representing broader perspectives, are asked during the learning cycles. This, in turn, can reduce the number of cycles required to fully learn, thereby improving its effectiveness and efficiency.
- *System and parametric design*: These concepts can provide a quick assessment of the impact of various design elements on other elements and can reduce negative impacts. For example, a more robust design can be developed in such a way that unexpected variation in the design will not have a negative impact on its performance.
- *Design of experiments (DOE)*: This involves the use of efficient and effective test strategies. Less testing is usually necessary than is typically required by traditional approaches in which one variable at a time is altered and the impact assessed through testing.

Background information on these and other tools are provided in the Appendix.

Performing Development Activities Concurrently

Traditional approaches to product development tend to be very sequential in nature. Systems designed based on "gates" tend to result in four to six major stages of product development. Very often there is a particular point at which a design is "frozen," and other activities are triggered, such as sourcing of materials and tooling. However, development processes designed on these principles do not always provide the short lead times that an organization is looking for. As long lead times continue, other problems can also plague the process (Figure 6.1).

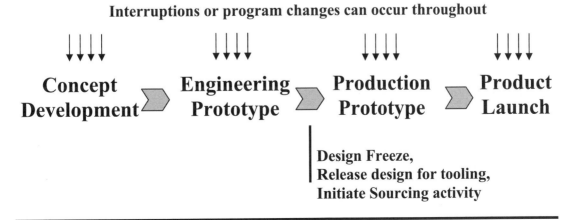

Figure 6.1   Sequential nature of traditional development processes.

For example, the longer the lead time, the more likely it is that interruptions or program or project changes will occur. Therefore, the management of the program or project becomes more complicated. Further, the sequential nature of traditional development processes tends *not* to promote "concurrent" or "simultaneous" design, in which suppliers, production, test, and other downstream participants are involved earlier in the process.

Lean Note

A "phased project planning" process has been practiced by some organizations, in some form, for decades. General Electric adopted such approaches, commonly known as "stage-gates," in the 1980s. Robert Cooper of McMaster University popularized this term and approach in the early 1990s in books and papers that describe a typical stage-gate process consisting of six stages and five gates. Since this time, numerous organizations, and Cooper himself, have worked to streamline this approach by removing one or three stages altogether.

Such approaches are not necessarily incorrect. In fact, great benefit can be realized by ensuring that specific information is available *before* moving on to the next stage or gate. These checkpoints can correct problems before they move on. Gate approaches tend to be results or milestone oriented, as opposed to process oriented. They also tend to be sequential in nature, which can slow the process, particularly at gates where there are inevitable delays in review and approval. Through experience, many organizations have developed ways to avoid some of these pitfalls.

The Toyota Product Development System makes tremendous use of "checklists" throughout their development process. The key is that they don't wait for a gate before they use them. Rather, they are an integrated part of the design process, used and maintained by the functional engineering managers themselves.

The Lean product development process is more concurrent. There are really just two phases—a learning or studying phase and an execution phase. During the study phase, multiple-designed product alternatives are assessed in parallel. The key is to learn as much as possible by exploring multiple alternatives before narrowing down solutions too quickly. This approach ensures involvement of suppliers, tool design, and production from the earliest stage of the study phase, another form of concurrency. Although this typically results in a longer study phase, the overall development lead time can be reduced significantly. This, in turn, provides other benefits to an organization. For example, there will be fewer interruptions through the life of the program or project.

Most organizations recognize the importance of involving other functions earlier in the design process, but few actually put this notion into practice. This can occur for several reasons:

■ Budgets, funding, etc.: For example, time for production personnel to be involved in the design process may never have been budgeted, nor funding provided, for this activity. This can be particularly the case in programs where funding is released by a controlling organization, as in a defense contract.
■ Sourcing practices: Most companies take a frozen drawing and solicit bids from several potential suppliers, often choosing the low-cost supplier. Such practices require a frozen design that typically is not available until much later in the process. It also makes it problematic to involve suppliers earlier. "We don't know who the supplier will be until the bid process is complete."
■ Historic behaviors: For example, production may be accustomed to fixing design problems once the product is in manufacturing. Therefore, there may be a reluctance to get involved earlier.

As you can see, these are three very big obstacles that get to the heart of an organization's supplier management, funding, and cultural issues. For example, a Lean development system can require a complete change in the relationship a company has with its suppliers. It requires true supplier partnering—committing to particular suppliers earlier in the development process in order to ensure their involvement sooner, and sticking by those commitments. Now, this may not represent as significant a change as many organizations might think at first. Most companies have a very good idea as to who they expect the supplier to be when they go out for bid. After all, there usually exists a substantial history with particular suppliers. The key is to recognize this fact, and make this a standard part of the Lean development system (Figure 6.2).

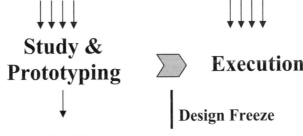

Fewer interruptions & program changes can occur with shorter lead times

Study & Prototyping ▷ **Execution**

| Design Freeze

Sourcing & Tool Design triggered, Process Capability considered throughout this phase

Figure 6.2 Concurrent nature of Lean development system.

Lean Note

James Morgan and Jeff Liker, in *The Toyota Product Development System* (2006), identified the two phases of Toyota's system. The *kentou*, or study phase, is meant to solve problems, resolve conflict, and very basically to learn. Here is where the most variability occurs, and Toyota seeks to segregate it from the rest of the product development process. Therefore, other participants can work on the execution phase with fewer interruptions.

It is during the *kentou* phase that multiple design alternatives are pursued. In 1995, Ward et al. coined the term, "set-based" concurrent engineering, to describe this approach. Tools have been developed to assess alternatives (e.g. trade-off curves).

Equally important, simultaneous engineering is performed during the *kentou* phase. In Toyota, this is typically accomplished by cross-functional module development teams (MDTs) that are not usually dedicated solely to a single program or project.

Mapping Tip:

An icon that is often used in many development processes is the "narrowing icon." It is used to show where decisions are made in the process with regard to alternate design solutions under consideration. In most development processes there are key points at which decisions are made to select which particular solutions will continue to be developed in subsequent stages, and which will be discarded. Guidelines to follow regarding the number of desired alternatives that should enter and exit this decision step, as well as the criteria for the narrowing, can be noted adjacent to the icon.

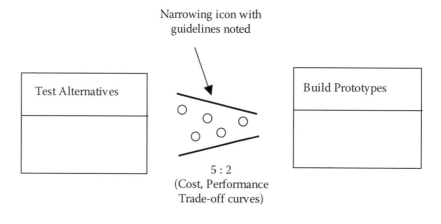

Distinguishing between "Good" Iterations and "Bad" Iterations

Many personnel involved in the design process focus on the iterative nature of product development, which they see as natural and inactionable. A Lean development process distinguishes between "good" and "bad" iterations. Bad iterations are rework loops. These represent pure waste and must be eliminated wherever possible. Checklists should be updated for use on future projects to prevent a reoccurrence of similar rework. Good iterations are when an organization learns. We want to speed these up without compromising their effectiveness.

We discussed the difference between knowledge creation and knowledge reuse previously. The more reuse of knowledge, the lower the chance for bad iterations. "Lessons learned" practices should be part of any development process. These lessons learned should identify time-consuming and costly iterations, and distinguish whether they were good or bad. To take these lessons and incorporate them into the design process to improve performance in the future, creative ideas must then be identified and acted on.

Maintaining a Process Focus Throughout

An important distinction between traditional and Lean development processes involves focus. Traditional approaches focus on process "outputs" rather than on process performance. Gate-oriented processes tend to perpetuate this focus because people simply want to "check off a box or boxes" in order to move on to the next stage. They often work on standardizing the output from stage to stage as opposed to determining *how* the stage was completed. For example, the question in a traditional approach is: "Did we get a prototype to pass by the designated milestone date?" A better question is: "What did we learn from our studies that can be shared with others in the organization, and could we have learned any more effectively or efficiently?" This is *not* a subtle point.

Organizations that continue to focus solely on outputs will never achieve the level of standardized work practices that are necessary to reduce the variability of an already variable process, and achieve sustainable results. This can have a strong behavioral impact. As an example, most engineers are pleased that a prototype passed testing, thereby avoiding the need for additional testing. A Lean design engineer wants to test to failure because more can be learned through failure.

The periodic revision of checklists used throughout the development process for the purpose of continually improving the system is just one example of the requisite process focus. The "lessons learned" practices are another. Many organizations have included some form of lessons learned activity toward the end of each development project. However, too often they are left incomplete, as development personnel are quickly assigned to the next project. Too often the lesson-learned activity deteriorates into a finger pointing exercise, thereby losing its purpose and benefits altogether. The key is to recognize that the development process is just that: A process that can be measured and continuously improved over time. Further, it must be an objective to reduce process variability, as discussed in chapter 2, whenever possible. In chapter 2, we noted that a large portion of the variability is created by organizations themselves.

> ### *Lean Example*
>
> Companies that have applied lean concepts to their development processes have implemented comprehensive sets of process performance measures including, but not limited to: average lead time per project, development cost per project, first pass yield or some other quality-related measures, and some measure of customer satisfaction. Other measures that have been implemented include: percentage reuse (where higher is better), projects in process (to monitor adherence to established pull system rules) as well as outcome-based measures, such as on time completion, and within target cost.

These are the key concepts upon which every Lean development system is based. There is also a myriad Lean development "tools" (as many as eighteen) that organizations should be familiar with, which can be used to improve the performance of the development process. Several are just variations of others—evolutions that have taken place over the years. The twelve most important tools are provided in the Appendix of this book. It is important to remember that these tools are a means to an end. An organization can apply all of the tools, and not necessarily have a Lean development process. Without inclusion of the key concepts described in this chapter, there is no guarantee for success.

The specific principles that underlie Lean development were well summarized by Morgan and Liker (2006) and are repeated in Table 6.1.

Table 6.1   Thirteen Principles of the Toyota Product Development System

Subsystem: Process

1. Establish customer-defined value to separate value add from waste.
2. Front-load the product development process to thoroughly explore alternative solutions while there is maximum design "space."
3. Create a leveled product development process flow.
4. Utilize rigorous standardization to reduce variation, and create flexibility and predictable outcomes.

Subsystem: Skilled People

5. Develop a Chief Engineer system to integrate development from start to finish.
6. Organize to balance functional expertise and cross-functional integration.
7. Develop towering technical competence in all engineers.
8. Fully integrate suppliers into the product development system.
9. Build in learning and continuous improvement.
10. Build a culture to support excellence and relentless improvement.

Subsystem: Tools and Technology

11. Adapt technology to fit your people and process.
12. Align your organization through simple, visual communication.
13. Use powerful tools for standardization and organizational learning.

In chapter 7, we will review the future state questions that embody Lean thinking and many of these specific principles. The reader will recognize that the process-oriented principles and those strongly related to process principles (e.g., learning and continuous improvement, supplier involvement) are embedded within the future state questions to be reviewed in the next chapter.

References

Morgan, J. and Liker, J. (2006) *The Toyota Product Development System*, Productivity Press, New York.

Ward, A., and Sobek, D. (1996) Principles from Toyota's set-based concurrent engineering process. *Proceedings of the 1996 ASME Design Engineering Technical Conference*, Irvine, CA.

Chapter 7

Creating the Future State Map

Future State Guidelines

The real power of value stream mapping lies in the creation of a future state based on Lean concepts. To do this effectively, there are guidelines that must be followed. These guidelines take the form of the seven future state questions. Together, the future state questions embody Lean thinking. In this chapter, we will explore each of these seven future state questions in depth, so that the reader can understand the intent of each. Collectively, the questions represent a thought process that will guide the team in identifying opportunities to apply Lean concepts and to design the future state. The future state questions are listed below.

- What does the customer really need?
- How often will we check our performance to customer needs?
- Which steps create value and which steps are waste?
- How can we flow work with fewer interruptions?
- How do we control work between interruptions, and how will work be triggered and prioritized?
- How will we level the workload and/or different activities?
- What process improvements will be necessary?

Although it is not necessary to go through the questions in this precise order, there is a reason that they are presented in this way. For example, because the customer's satisfaction is paramount, we must always start with: "What does the customer really need?" Further, we always want to ask the "waste question" before we ask the "flow question." We certainly wouldn't want to flow waste.

> ### *Mapping Tip*
>
> Too often, value stream mapping teams take a brainstorming approach to develop the future state. Dozens of Post-it® notes are placed on the current state map. Although this approach might generate many ideas, other problems will likely result. First, often the underlying structure of the development process remains unchanged because only point solutions are identified. Next, few organizations can support the successful implementation of dozens of product development improvement projects. Instead, the team should identify twelve or so key improvement projects that they will focus on over the next year or less.
>
> Still another pitfall to the brainstorming approach is the inability to carefully assess the impact of particular ideas on lead time, quality, or cost. Such assessments are needed to prioritize the improvement projects. Finally, there remains the possibility that the key Lean concepts of value, flow, pull, and perfection will be overlooked in the brainstorming process. Brainstorming does take place during the development of the future state, but always in the context of the seven questions.

Before exploring the future state questions, we will review a key ground rule for developing a future state map. The most important ground rule is the "70 percent and keep updating" rule. If the team believes that they have a 70 percent chance of implementing a particular idea in less than one year, and certainly in one to six months, it should include the idea as part of the future state. This ground rule serves several purposes:

■ The team will *not* have 100 percent certainty that all ideas identified during the design of the future state will be achievable. Although this is to be expected, teams can get caught up by this fact, the creative process squelched, and progress impeded. The facilitator should use the 70 percent rule to get the team to record the idea in the form of a "kaizen burst" (a short burst of activity) and move forward.

> ### *Mapping Tip:*
>
> Specific improvement efforts agreed upon by the team are recorded on the Future State map by use of the kaizen burst icon. It represents an action that must be completed in order to make the Future State a reality. Therefore, the numerous kaizen bursts will be used to develop an Implementation Plan. This will be covered in more detail in Chapter 9.
>
> Kaizen burst icon with description within ⟶ Cross functional Design Team

- The team must design a future state that is achievable in a reasonable timeframe. Less than one year is considered reasonable. Even still, real changes must be made in even shorter timeframes, say, one to six months. If the organization does not see any benefits for long periods of time, the entire improvement effort will suffer. The facilitator should ask, "Can we implement that idea in one to six months? In six to twelve months?"
- The previous point underscores the need to have the team develop creative ideas to improve the development process. The team cannot simply rely on ideas that will take long periods of time to implement (greater than one year). An attempt to Lean the development process by implementing new engineering computer-based software and systems, which can take two or more years to fully implement, will result in unacceptable delays in the short term. Although Engineering may indeed need such a system in the long term, the facilitator should always ask, "What can we do to help things over the next one to six months? The next six to twelve months?"

Now let's explore each future state question in the order that they have been presented.

What Does the Customer Really Need?

The creation of the future state must always begin with this question. No future state can be developed for any process or value stream without first considering the customer and his/her needs. Assumptions can be dangerous and should be avoided at all costs. Rather, the best way to identify the customer's true needs is to *involve* the customer in the development of the future state in some way. To help with this critical first step, we offer these follow-up questions.

- Ask who needs the output (or product) of the process. Make certain to identify *everyone* who may make use of the output of the development process. Don't ignore the numerous and important *internal* customers of the development process, such as Production and Purchasing.
- What do they need? Get specific input at this point. Ask the customer to distinguish between what they *want* and what they really *need*.
- When do they need it? This will determine the overall desired lead time as well as the specific point in the process that particular information is needed.
- What demand is expected on the development process in the future?

To put it another way, what "service level" does the customer need? There are several aspects of a service level—lead time, quality, and cost—and the concept can be applied to both internal and external customers. First, let's answer this question in the context of external customers. What is the desired lead time for the development process? The answer, typically driven by the market, will be a key design parameter of the future state.

Second, what is the expected quality level of the output? In other words, we need to define an outcome that will meet the needs of customers and deliver the value that they expect. How will this be defined and measured as a regular part of the future state process? Clearly, an effective "voice of the customer" process must be part of our future state design.

Certainly, an important aspect of perceived value is price. In most cases, the market sets the pricing. Companies then must try to meet a particular cost—a target cost—that will result in a product or service with an acceptable gross margin. A cost model must be developed in order to continually track the expected product or service cost versus the target cost. Remember that design is a trade-off process. Numerous trade-offs analyses will be performed throughout the development process, trade-offs in terms of performance and cost. Therefore, a cost model must be part of our future state design if it is not a practice used in the current state. Although most companies attempt some form of cost modeling in the design process, they often overlook several significant contributors to cost. A template for such a model is provided in the Appendix: "Lean Development Tools."

We can also apply the same questions in the context of internal customers. For example, what specific information does Purchasing need to initiate its sourcing process, and when do they need it in order to have sufficient time to accomplish this important task effectively? When we ask this question for each of the key internal customers, we can identify several key milestones within the overall lead time defined to satisfy the external customer (Figure 7.1).

In Figure 7.1, we show the overall lead time upon which the entire process will be predicated. Within that lead time, we can define when particular functions, such as Purchasing or Production, need to start their activities in order to ensure that overall lead time goals will be met. Difficult questions will arise

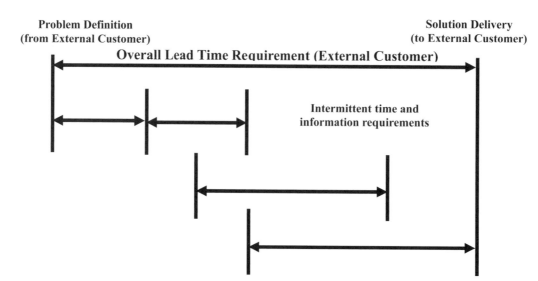

Figure 7.1 Defining requirements for external and internal customers.

during this discussion as different functions compete for time. Of course, performing activities in parallel whenever possible will help to minimize the overall lead time. As previously discussed, concurrency is an important Lean product development concept.

Throughout the development of the future state, current beliefs and practices will be challenged. For example, particular functions may believe that they need more time than they really do. They also may feel that they must wait for the availability of particular information before they can initiate their activities—much later than is really necessary. To ensure clarity throughout the organization then, the specific information needs of each internal customer must be clearly defined. Once again, existing practices and beliefs must be challenged. For example, Purchasing personnel might believe that they need a completed design, released by Engineering, in order to initiate the sourcing process for tooling. However, in reality they can initiate this process much earlier, if they involve the supplier in creative ways. As we discussed previously, involving suppliers earlier in the development process is a critical Lean product development concept and, therefore, must be part of our future state design.

Lean Example

When we examine the supplier's process, we often find that a large portion of its lead time lies in the purchase of raw material. A supplier does not require a detailed, released drawing to initiate purchase of steel to make the tool. He simply needs a general concept, which is available early in the development process. If the company simply provides this information to the supplier earlier, significant time can be reduced from the supplier's lead time, and, of course, the overall development time. At one company, this resulted in a twelve-week reduction. Such a practice will often require companies to work much differently with suppliers than is the case with traditional practices.

We must be assured that the "service level" in terms of lead time, quality, and cost will be met consistently over time. Of course, engineers can design anything, given enough time and money. Unfortunately, these resources are limited. If the resources involved in the development process do not have the ability to consistently meet the lead time, quality, and cost expectations over time, the result will be an ineffective process. The most common reason that an organization and its development resources cannot meet expectations is that demands on their time exceed capacity. Therefore, we must understand the degree of demand on the development process. How many development projects are expected over a period of time? Will there be variation in the demand for any particular reason, such as seasons or industry shows? If so, how will the increase in demand be met? Although it is not important to answer the "how" question at this time, it is important to understand the demand itself and the variation of demand on the development process.

We can express customer demand in terms of "Takt time." Takt time is calculated by dividing the effective working time in a period by the demand on the process for the same period. If we express demand in terms of a day, then the effective working time must be in terms of a day. We could express it in terms of a week, a month, a year, or a season, whatever is appropriate. Once Takt time has been determined, we can then turn to balancing the pace of processing to meet the pace of demand.

Takt time = Effective working time in a period ÷ Demand in a period

---

Lean Note

Takt is a German word that means "a precise interval of time." The term originated in the field of music—a musical meter. It was first used in production management in the 1930s in the German aircraft industry and was widely used by Toyota starting in the 1950s and 1960s. Takt time is used to synchronize or balance the pace of processing with the pace of demand. While people now understand its application to production processes, there still exist difficulties in applying it to information and development processes. This occurs because people do not fully understand its real purpose.

How do we use Takt time? Let's say that the desired lead time to complete design projects is one week, and one week is equivalent to forty hours—a one-shift design process. Now, let's say we currently have three projects that need to be completed. However, the projects vary considerably in terms of complexity. Project "A" requires forty hours, and Project "B" requires ten hours. A third project, Project "C" requires approximately thirty hours to complete (Figure 7.2).

Project	Estimated Hours
A	40
B	10
C	30
Total	80 hours

Figure 7.2   Development process Takt time.

Is the number of projects required per week a good expression of demand? On the contrary, the number of hours of work to be completed during the week is a better expression of demand on the resources expected to complete the work. In this example, there are eighty hours of work to be completed within the forty-hour service level. What does this tell you regarding the resources necessary to complete the work? We would need two people to meet the demand and maintain the defined service level. This example illustrates the need to have a capacity planning tool for key design resources. We do not want some complex capacity planning tool that is difficult to maintain and manage over time, but rather something very simple. Such a tool must be a part of the future state design. In this, we will be able to monitor demand versus capacity. We will be able to identify situations where demand exceeds capacity and, thereby, impacts the flow of projects. Of course, we can identify the opposite situation as well.

We can also compare Takt time directly to process time in order to determine the required resources or capacities for each step, or entire processes. Constraints or "bottlenecks" in the current state can be identified through the use of Takt time. The means to do this depends on the ability to define demand in a way that relates to the work content for particular processes (see Lean Examples below for further illustration). In addition, understanding the resource requirements for each major activity may lead to a reconsideration of current roles and responsibilities in order to improve flow.

Lean Example

At one "Design-to-Order" company, two design teams were put in place to meet overall demand and maintain established service levels. However, given the variability in orders, either team could find itself "overloaded" at any particular time. To alleviate undue stress on either team and increase efficiency, the company posted a dry-erase board for each team, displaying their current work load in hours versus their capacity. The boards were updated as projects were completed and new ones added. New projects were assigned to each team by Sales personnel based on the status of projects displayed on their respective boards, each of which took fewer than five minutes per day to update. At another company, the unit of measure used was dollars (the dollar value of the order). Within this particular company, the dollar value of the order directly related to the amount of work needed to complete the design. This information was readily available at time of order entry.

Determining meaningful Takt times is important as we identify an appropriate management timeframe for the various development processes within the enterprise. This leads us into our next future state question.

Lean Example

At an avionics company, on comparison of the Takt time or demand rate to the various process times in the current state, it was apparent that the constraint in the development system was the particular Engineering technical expertise. The easy answer would be to hire another person for this role. However, a better approach was to identify means to streamline the activities of this role and to shift particular activities to less constrained roles. This allowed the company to resolve the existing bottleneck without the need for additional resources. At first, this approach was not deemed possible because initial beliefs held that only a person of particular experience and skill could fulfill this role. However, on further examination, it was clear that numerous activities could be off-loaded to other people within the organization who possessed less experience and other skills. Development lead time was reduced by approximately two to four weeks from a current twenty-four weeks. Further, it relieved a lot of frustration and stress within the current system.

How Often Will We Check Performance?

The frequency with which a company checks performance is often referred to as "management timeframe" or "pitch." How long does the organization want to wait before it realizes that it is not processing development projects in a timely manner? For the example in Figure 7.2, we would certainly not wait until the end of the week to discover that we have a problem; valuable time would be lost forever. Lean enterprises have very short management timeframes. They quickly recognize when goals are not being met and respond accordingly to correct the situation. What frequency is appropriate for the example provided in Figure 7.2? Given the one-week service level, perhaps a daily review would be appropriate.

Lean Note

In a Lean enterprise, the management timeframe is significantly less than that of traditional organizations. How much should it be reduced? That depends on Takt time and the level of responsiveness that can be achieved in the future state. In general, the shorter the lead time and the greater the number of design projects, the shorter the management timeframe or "pitch" (i.e., the higher the frequency of review).

Clarification is necessary to distinguish between setting milestones and the frequency of reviewing the status of the system. Milestones are events, typically when a task is completed. We don't usually want to wait until a milestone has not been met to identify a problem. Once again, valuable time will have been lost. With management timeframe or pitch, we review the system at a set frequency—daily, weekly, or within some other period of time.

We want a simple, visual way—a "Takt image"—of determining whether or not we are meeting the service levels established for lead time, quality, and even cost. We don't want to spend a lot of nonvalue-added time checking on the system. Traditional development systems typically include periodic status meetings that require one to two hours to conduct. We certainly don't want more meetings. An easier way to identify potential problems that may jeopardize meeting the established service level must be identified and be part of the future state. Companies have developed creative visual means to provide Takt image. Many possibilities exist.

- Design personnel could "raise a flag," literally, at their office or cubicle that would trigger the manager to ask what the problem is, and initiate corrective action.
- The design team might hold ten minute-long morning huddles in the workplace (at the *gemba,* where the work is performed) around a dry erase board that displays project status.

Whatever technique is used to provide Takt image, it is almost always worker managed. The people involved in the design process will provide the status and trigger action, when necessary. The manner in which management responds is the real key.

This is a key component of the Lean product development process that must be well understood. What action will be taken if the service levels are not being met or are in jeopardy of not being met?

Providing assistance, getting personally involved to resolve a problem, perhaps calling a team meeting to determine an appropriate course of action are all acceptable responses. The root causes must quickly be identified and corrective action taken immediately to return to the desired service level. For instance, if a spike occurred in the number of projects received, additional resources can be brought in from other areas to meet this temporary change in demand. What is not acceptable is a response that if not in words, but in actions states, "Just work faster or harder."

Lean Example

The engineering manager at one company wanted to improve flow and reduce lead time of the design process. In the past, the manager held meetings every two weeks to determine the status of the various design efforts in process through "percent to complete" estimates from the engineers. However, scheduled completion dates continued to slip. To correct this, the manager determined the Takt time in terms of engineering hours required per period (e.g., a week). He established a management timeframe or pitch of two days. Then he broke demand into blocks of time equivalent to the pitch. Tasks with an expected completion time of two days were assigned to the various engineering resources. Progress was reviewed every two days to determine if the goals were being met. If not, action was taken (e.g., resources or tasks were reassigned). This was accomplished by a simple flag system, whereby the manager walked through the office every two days within the space of approximately fifteen minutes. The results were far beyond what was expected. A nearly 50 percent reduction in lead time was achieved. This was attributed to the short-term goal setting tied to specific tangible deliverables; periodic adjustment of the system as necessary; and *less* work-in-process, which allowed resources to focus on fewer activities at a time. At another company, dry erase boards using "traffic light" techniques clearly showed the status of a project. For a project meeting expectations for the various stages of processing, a green magnet was placed next to it; for a project that was in jeopardy of not meeting expectations, a yellow magnet was placed; or for a project that was *not* currently going to meet expectations, a red magnet was placed. The members of the development team managed the visual signals.

Lean Note

There is a belief that precise data are required to adequately capacity plan a development process. However, with shorter management timeframes, a more robust development system can be implemented that can deal with unforeseen capacity issues in a timely and effective manner. In the preceding Lean Example, the manager was reluctant to break demand into the two day blocks for fear that he would estimate incorrectly. This was a pointless concern because he would know this fact within two days and be able to react accordingly.

At this point, the value stream mapping team has identified key aspects of the management system that will be implemented as part of the new development process. We will now move on to the next future state question.

Which Steps Create Value and Which Are Waste?

Of course, we must ask this question: Which steps create value and which are waste? A review of the current state map will facilitate the discussion around this question. The wastes should be very clear, although we may not, in the past, have considered many of the steps to be nonvalue-added. Some helpful subquestions to prompt the discussion include:

- Is there any evidence of "overprocessing" waste? Are customer requirements clearly understood?
- Are we reinventing the proverbial wheel? Do design personnel have ready access to previous designs that can be reused? Is it easy to locate and retrieve this information?
- Are particular elements of the design completed too early?
- Is there evidence that significantly development personnel are following different practices? If so, what impact does it have on the current state? Does it take some people longer to perform particular tasks?
- What is the accuracy and completeness of the information as it passes from process to process? What do the percent complete and accurate figures tell you? How about the first pass yield? What would be some root causes for such problems? Is it simple awareness of the needs of subsequent process steps?
- Iterations may indicate the need for rework and be another symptom of waste. The iteration icon will highlight where in the value stream these currently occur.
- Where do interruptions in the flow of information occur? The inbox queue icons will be indicators of such disruptions. What would be some potential root causes for these interruptions? Often these occur due to some variability in the process. Is there any way to reduce this variability?
- Do particular activities wait on upstream processes for required information? Are particular design elements completed too late?
- Is there evidence of significant hand-offs? With each hand-off comes the opportunity for a queue to form as well as information to be incorrectly passed on or received.
- What knowledge and skill is truly required to perform particular tasks? There may be other issues created by the current definition of roles and responsibilities, and how work is divided along the development process. Perhaps the number of hand-offs can be reduced by reconsidering existing roles and responsibilities.

As we mentioned in chapter 3, information quality-related issues are often the focus of the first future state or states. The use of checklists throughout the development process is a part of nearly every future state, since they help improve information quality, and can be quickly and easily implemented. In addition, another focus tends to be on standard work: identifying standard design practices and providing specific design standards that must be adhered to. Identifying methods to improve flow will be the subject of the next future state question.

How Can We Flow Work with Fewer Interruptions?

Figure 7.3 depicts the significant benefits of flow processing versus batch and queue processing. In the bottom figure, all of the queues have been eliminated or, at least, minimized. Lead time can be significantly reduced by 50 to

Functional, Batch & Queue Processing

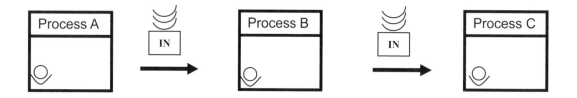

Cross-functional, Flow Processing

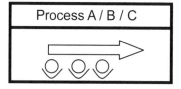

Figure 7.3   Batch and queue versus flow processing.

90 percent as the queues are eliminated or minimized. Quality of the process can improve by 30 to 90 percent, and process time can be reduced by as much as 40 percent by improving the flow of information through the development process.

How can the queues be eliminated or minimized to improve flow through the system? There are numerous approaches that can be explored. What does the bottom graphic in Figure 7.3 imply? Perhaps cross-functional teams dedicated to a particular project or projects can help to improve flow. To support this concept, maybe the team members should be co-located or located in close proximity to each other. Of course, the advantages and disadvantages of such an approach must be explored. Another alternative might be to bring "shared resources" together periodically to complete various development activities as well as to communicate the status of projects in process. Recently, the term *obeya* (or "big room") has been used to describe the forum in which cross-functional team members can work together on development projects. The concept dates back many years and has been used on large design projects, such as aerospace and naval ships.

The key is to improve communication among the functions in order to improve the flow of information. The manner in which this occurs depends on the circumstances that the company faces. For example, the number and current location of resources involved in the development process may warrant one approach over another. Are we talking about co-locating twelve people or twelve hundred? Other factors, such as the complexity and duration of projects, and the number of projects in process at any time, must also be considered.

Lean Example

Different industries have established multifunctional product development teams organized in production-like "cells" in order to realize the significant benefits of uninterrupted flow (i.e., reduced lead time, improved quality, greater flexibility). An aerospace company reduced overall design lead time by dedicating functional resources to specific product value streams, and co-locating the various functions: product design, tool design, process engineering, contract management, production planning, even purchasing. The result was a 60 to 75 percent decrease in lead time. At a shipbuilder, numerous cross-functional teams were co-located based on the manner in which the ship was to be built ("modules"). Members included various engineering functions, quality assurance personnel, tooling design, and production engineers. Systems engineers oversaw the design activities to ensure necessary integration of the module design. While still in progress, this effort is demonstrating a 50 to 60 percent reduction in development lead time.

"Shared resources" can develop the potential for interruptions in flow. Development resources must have ready access to the tools that they need, particularly as they try to reduce the lead time for the learning cycles within the development process. Design engineers need the ability to quickly assess ideas and their impact on the design as well as on the production process. Therefore, they need access to production and test equipment, and to other tools. While 3D modeling is one tool that can help to assess the impact of a design change on other design elements, it is often limited in terms of the amount of learning that can be achieved. For example, it may not provide insight on the impact on production. Other tools must be provided in order to eliminate this form of potential interruption, and the availability of needed resources must be a part of the future state design.

Lean Example

At one company, an oven with measurement equipment was placed on a cart that could be wheeled right to the engineer's desk to allow for experimentation to be performed. Several of these carts were assembled and made available to the engineers. Previous to this, they had to schedule time in a test lab that was also supporting production. At another company, the engineers had their own mock-up shop stocked with simple materials, such as wood, Styrofoam™, etc. They could fabricate mock-ups of the product as well as the equipment that might be required to produce the product. This allows design personnel to go beyond brainstorming ideas and move to trystorming where maximum learning is achieved.

Lean Note

Although Toyota relies on shared resources throughout its development process, with the exception of the chief engineer (CE) and the CE's staff, who are dedicated to specific projects, this approach requires tremendous planning and discipline to be successful. For less disciplined organizations, dedicated design teams making use of development lines, testing equipment, and such may be the way to go to avoid the conflict of shared resources, and to ensure the availability of resources when needed.

Lean Note

A common impediment to flow is not just the availability of resources (in other words, the timing of availability of shared resources), but the overall capacity of particular resources. Often true resource constraints are discovered in the current state map. While it is usually not news for the people performing the work, it seems to be a surprise to functional management. Furthermore, particular resources may be loaded at or near capacity. This, too, can create flow problems because there is little or no way to respond when problems such as rework iterations occur. Key resources should only be loaded to 80 to 85 percent of capacity in order to provide adequate flexibility.

Another potential cause for interruption may be the existing batch practices that affect the flow of information. These must be addressed and resolved. What are the potential advantages and disadvantages of designing a product in smaller elements or, perhaps, releasing specific elements of designs yet to be completed to other functions, so that they may initiate their activities? Earlier in this chapter, we provided an example of how this might work with suppliers. Perhaps there are similar advantages for Production, Testing, and other downstream functions. It may allow for particular development activities to be performed concurrently or simultaneously.

Concurrent Engineering, as discussed in chapter 6, is an important flow concept and opportunities to do such must be identified as part of the future state design. It is typically during discussion of this future state question that such opportunities are specifically identified. In the case of a manufacturer, it is desirable to develop the new product with a keen awareness of existing production capabilities. Manufacturing standards must be identified by Production and adhered to by designers throughout the development process. In a situation in which a new production process is required, the new process should be developed concurrently with the product, if at all possible. There are usually significant opportunities to reduce lead time and development cost by the application of concurrent or simultaneous engineering concepts.

"One piece flow" (or working on one design project at a time) is an important concept to consider (Figure 7.4). Clearly, the figure on the left, in which design personnel can focus on one project or task at a time, depicts the ideal situation. This approach usually results in improved effectiveness and efficiency as well as improved quality performance. It is also an easier process to manage. Consider the situation in which multiple projects are being worked on at the same time. Now, consider what happens when a problem arises with one project. That one problem will have a negative impact on the other projects, tasks, or activities in process. Engineers will push those projects aside in order to catch up on the problematic project or task. This practice can then create problems with the other projects, in all probability extending their lead times. This kind of snowball effect requires greater management skills to correct.

If "one piece flow" is possible, the only interruption or queue that must be carefully managed is at the very beginning of the process (Figure 7.5). Certainly, most would agree that an interruption is easier to manage at one point in the process than at multiple points.

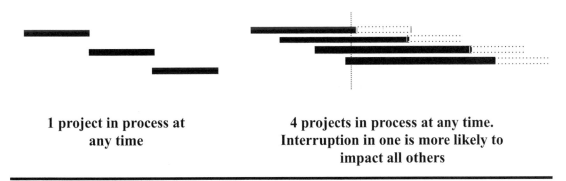

1 project in process at any time

4 projects in process at any time. Interruption in one is more likely to impact all others

Figure 7.4 One project at a time versus multiple projects.

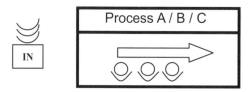

Figure 7.5 Single queue at beginning of process.

So, can "one piece flow" be achieved? It certainly becomes more possible as lead time is significantly reduced and sources of process variability are addressed. However, it is not always possible due to interruptions in the design process that cannot be addressed, and where work must stop and wait. Examples of such interruptions include waiting for customer approval or regulatory approval, but other examples exist as well. The main consideration is whether all of the significant interruptions to flow can be eliminated and, if not, where the remaining ones occur in the development process. We will have more discussion of interruptions in the next future state question.

How Do We Control Work between Interruptions? How Will Work Be Triggered and Prioritized?

Perhaps the best we can achieve are several "pockets of flow." We can expect that flow will stop and queuing will occur at particular points (Figure 7.6). If we do not address how the queues will be managed, other problems may need to be dealt with at this point. First, how will we control the flow of work to and from a queue? A means to link the processes before and after the interruption must be implemented as part of the future state.

How do we control the size of the queue so that it does not grow beyond what is easily managed? If we control the release of work and "pull" the work through only when the downstream resources are available, we can maintain a more predictable process and probably a more effective and efficient one. We can establish a standard work-in-process level between processes and then provide simple visual means to monitor these queues. The queues could be monitored per the existing management timeframe or pitch, or in some cases in near real time. In other words, basic pull systems can be implemented to control the queue, and

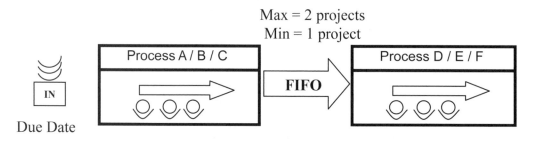

Figure 7.6 Pockets of flow with queues in between.

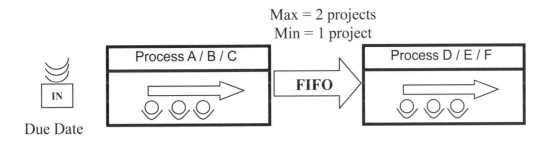

Figure 7.7 First-in-first-out (FIFO) lanes.

should be part of our future state design. Pull systems are really just decision-making tools that control the flow of resources (e.g., information, materials, etc.).

If the queue grows to a certain point, this may be an indication that more resources are needed and that demand is exceeding capacity at that moment. Additional resources may need to be identified, trained, and made available for such situations. Perhaps resources can be "pulled" within the organization or from outside. Certainly the upstream process should not continue to "push" information into the queue. If they cannot lend assistance to the downstream process, then they should work on other activities until they receive a signal to resume.

Another issue that can arise when queues are present involves the prioritization of work. How do we maintain consistent priorities throughout the value stream when interruptions occur? What is the desired prioritization of the queue? Typically, the release of work at the very beginning of the development process is based on due date or on a first-in-first-out (FIFO) basis. The desired sequence throughout the rest of the development process is FIFO. There may be situations when this is not the desired sequence, but it is the most common practice. This is depicted in Figure 7.7.

Lean Note

"Pull" processing is a method of control in which downstream activities signal their needs to upstream activities. Pull processing strives to eliminate overproduction. Nothing is processed by the upstream supplier process until the downstream customer process signals a need. This is the opposite of "push" production.

There are three basic types of pull production systems:

1. Supermarket Pull Systems, where an amount of each material is stored.
2. Sequential Pull Systems (FIFO) where products are made-to-order. Such systems are used when there are too many part numbers to hold inventory of each in a supermarket.
3. Mixed Systems, which use a combination of the first two systems.

We want to control the flow of information and people resources in the development process. While the concept of "supermarkets" may not easily apply, the other form of pull system (e.g., sequential) most certainly does.

How much work (e.g., projects, hours) is appropriate in the development value stream at any time? In other words, how much work will be triggered? The answer is: as little as possible while still meeting demand and the lead time goals for the future state. It really depends on the location and duration of the interruption. For interruptions, such as customer approval, waiting for outside testing to be completed, or regulatory agency approval (e.g., Federal Drug Administration [FDA], Federal Aviation Administration [FAA]), the interruption can be significant; to avoid wasted time and capacity, these types of interruptions would warrant more work or projects in the system at any time. However, such interruptions often occur toward the end of the design process and, therefore, "one piece flow" can be followed up to this point before a second project is kicked off. Nearly all of the work will have been completed at this time, including production process development, if done correctly. Starting a second project should have minimal impact on flow and predictability.

Lean Example

At a clothing company, the demand was for forty-eight new designs per year, or twelve new designs per season. Toward the end of the development process for each design, there was a "batch" approval process. This process was performed once per month and there was no changing it. Given this situation, the amount of work to be triggered was determined to be four designs. Only four designs would be in process at any time. Previously, there were as many as twelve, which added variability to the process and decreased predictability of flow. The new practice also resulted in "leveling," or evenly distributing, the development process throughout the season, thereby reducing the end of season "crunch" that was experienced for years.

The number of projects to be triggered is not always the primary concern. More important is the *time equivalent* of those projects with regard to work content. Therefore, other units of measure, such as hours, may need to be considered. As a result, the "batch size" of design may need to be reconsidered. Although many people involved in the development process do not view their work as a batch, the amount of work in terms of time does, in fact, represent a batch. For example, is design releasing one hundred hours worth of design work at a time or one thousand hours? If design engineers are releasing in large amounts, what is the impact on lead time? Quality? Cost? What if we tied the batch size to the management timeframe or pitch discussed in a previous Lean Example? How would this impact the process?

> ### *Lean Example*
>
> A common pull system often used within the development process involves the use of external Engineering resources to supplement capacity. The key is to have set rules that will trigger the pull of external resources when the queue at the beginning of the development process grows beyond an established amount and warrants such. The need for standard work is especially important in this scenario.

Another form of potential interruption is when unplanned disruptions occur. Our entire discussion thus far on this future state question has involved planned or known disruptions. However, nonstandard conditions can occur at unforeseen times, which in turn can interrupt flow. For example, what will happen if incorrect information is found? What will happen if a design concept fails to perform as expected? Processes to respond to such occurrences must be defined. It may require cross-functional involvement to correct the situation and reinstitute flow. Certainly, we will want to address these issues as quickly as possible and not wait for the next design review meeting.

When such situations occur, the process has failed in some way. Therefore, these situations represent learning opportunities. A "lessons learned" process (see chapter 6)—effective and efficient, of course—needs to be a part of our future state design. Perhaps a change in an existing checklist will be needed to prevent the situation from recurring. In the meantime, some reallocation of resources will be needed to get the project back on "pitch."

The "lessons learned" process most often used is a "line stop" concept where a problem is identified and escalated to a cross-functional team. The team will understand the root cause of the problem, identify possible preventive measures, and work to implement these agreed-upon measures. It is basically a "plan-do-check-act" cycle that is followed to continuously improve the development process. A Lean enterprise sees nonstandard conditions as a means to improve the process, therefore, these conditions should be readily identified by people involved in the development process rather than worked around or kept hidden. Some form of line stop practice, in which the process is temporarily stopped when problems arise, and opportunities to improve the development process identified, should be part of the future state design.

How Will We Level the Workload and Mix of Activities?

Since the nature and volume of work can vary greatly in a development process, this question is highly relevant. We have discussed and addressed a range of causes for variability during the future state design so far. However, there are some other situations that we have not yet discussed in depth, such as

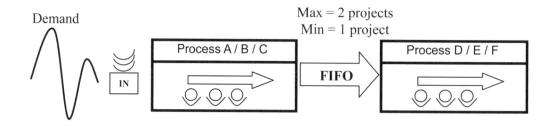

Figure 7.8 The impact of unlevel demand is reduced by FIFO (first-in-first-out) lanes.

leveling. There are two aspects of leveling: the volume of work and the mix of activities.

First is a discussion on the volume of work. Perhaps the demand on development resources varies due to seasonality or other causes. For example, in some industries there is the big show every year where new products are introduced to the market. This can create unlevel demand on the system as many design projects are all due around the same time. Therefore, some method of leveling design work through the year must be implemented and included in the future state design. Cooperation of multiple functions will be necessary to effectively level the development activity. Sales and Marketing personnel must support this effort. While not easy, leveling can have a significant and positive impact on the development system. The pull systems described in the previous future state question and the control of the release of work to the system, will ensure that the unlevel demand will not negatively impact the development process, as shown Figure 7.8. However, the queue on the front end still must be managed.

Lean Example

For years at a furniture company, there was an annual crunch time as new product designs had to be completed in time for the big annual industry show. Approximately seventy new products were needed for the show. The development manager of the company calculated a Takt time of .7 weeks (50 weeks to design 70 new styles), meaning that a new design had to be completed every .7 weeks, or that 1.4 designs needed to be completed per week. The manager then set the goal for the entire development process to complete 1.5 designs each week in order to level the work load throughout the year. The organization was able to avoid the last minute rush that they had experienced for years. An additional, unforeseen benefit is that this practice of leveling gave the company the ability to introduce new styles throughout the year. The company was better able to respond to market conditions in a timely manner. For example, perhaps a style did not sell as expected; new styles could quickly be introduced.

In addition, organizations should really work to identify potential root causes for this demand variability and determine if any are actionable. In other words, can some creative ideas be identified to level the demand itself on the development process? Organizations have been surprised at times to learn that they themselves may be creating some of this variation.

Now let's talk about the "mix" of development work. This can take many forms. Does the complexity of designs vary enough that it will have a negative impact on the future state envisioned? If so, maybe this represents multiple service families, as was discussed in chapter 1. In this case, we may need several development processes, each designed to handle projects of a particular range of complexity. Does the future state design need to change in any way? Perhaps we do not want to precisely schedule by due date or on a FIFO basis, particularly at the beginning of the process. It may be advantageous to release the work based on complexity, e.g., easy project, difficult project, easy project, and so on. This may help to level the development system. Of course, it may not always be possible to maintain this desired "mix" over time. But, if it can help most of the time, it should be considered when designing the future state.

Another concern may involve response or lead time. All along, we have been designing for a particular lead time for the development process. Do you envision projects that will have to be "fast tracked?" If so, how will they be handled? It should be noted that the number of "rush" designs should decrease with shorter development lead times. Nevertheless, there may still be the need to quickly complete particular designs.

Lean Example

A company identified the need to fast track a particular design. In order to provide this ability without overly complicating the development system, a "holely" FIFO lane was implemented. If the maximum allowed in the FIFO lane at any time was four projects, no more than three were kept there, leaving one slot for any fast track projects. The fast track projects were then placed at the front of all downstream FIFO lanes. They were placed in a red folder to clearly identify them. Certainly, such quick response ability can be enhanced, if needed, if the development system is designed and loaded at 80 to 85 percent of capacity, as we previously recommended.

To summarize, a robust development system can be designed with particular features to meet unique needs, if these needs are identified and discussed as part of the future state design.

What Process Improvements Will Be Necessary?

Various process improvements were probably identified during discussion of the first six questions. These would be recorded on the future state map using the "kaizen burst" icon. However, the team may have overlooked particular improvements. The purpose of this question is to take a step back and identify anything important that may be missing. A word of caution: the team should *not* be attempting to identify any and all process improvements. Remember, the goal is not quantity, but quality. The important thing to ask at this point is: "Have we overlooked any important process improvements that will keep us from achieving the future state envisioned?" The team will add several kaizen bursts, as necessary.

In the next chapter, the future state questions will be applied to the DevelopTek case study.

Reference

Morgan, J. and Liker, J. (2006), *Toyota Product Development System*, Productivity Press, New York.

Chapter 8

DevelopTek's Future State

We will now apply the seven future state questions to the DevelopTek case study. The future state to be developed in this chapter is just one of several possible future state designs. More important than the specifics of the future state design is the use of the future state questions to facilitate the discussion to apply Lean thinking and associated concepts to the development process.

What does the Customer Really Need?

As previously stated, DevelopTek's market requires a ninety-day lead time for the development of new products. To recall, the lead time of the current state is one hundred forty-three to one hundred sixty-three days, and as much as one hundred ninety-three days when several redesign iterations are required. Therefore, DevelopTek needs to eliminate at least seventy-three days from the current state in order to achieve the desired lead time. In addition, the number of projects requiring redesign, as well as the number of redesign iterations, must be reduced in order to more consistently meet the desired lead time. The team really should target a lead time of less than ninety days (say, seventy-five days) in order to better ensure that the desired lead time can be met. Specific ideas to reduce lead time will be explored during discussion of subsequent future state questions.

From a quality standpoint, the value stream mapping (VSM) team has established as a goal a 50 percent reduction in warranty costs—from 6% of sales to 3%. In addition, they established a goal for first pass yield of 70%, up from 8%. The team felt strongly that these goals could be met within the next twelve months. Once again, methods to improve the quality performance of the development process will be identified during discussion of subsequent future state questions. The quality expectations, together with the desired lead time, will form the service level for the future state. All of the VSM team's efforts in designing the future state will be geared toward meeting this service level.

After establishing their goal for the first pass yield, the team next calculated a Takt time for the development process as follows:

Takt Time = 52 weeks per year ÷ 26 projects per year = 2 weeks per project

If we assume a five-day work week, the Takt time will be ten days per project. In other words, the development process must have the capacity to complete a project every ten days, and development projects must be completed within ninety days from start to finish. The Takt time can be compared to the total process time of the current development process to determine the amount of resources required. To do this, we will assume an eight-hour workday. Therefore, Takt time can be restated as eighty hours per project (ten days per project × eight hours per day). From the current state map, the total process time is estimated to be four hundred thirty-two hours.

Number of required people = 432 people-hours per project ÷ 80 hours = 5.4 people

In other words, if nothing else changes, approximately five to six people will be required to meet demand. Of course, there is much waste in the current process, and the expectation will be to reduce process time and, in turn, the number of people required. The number of required resources must be reassessed as the VSM team continues its future state design, and as ideas are generated to reduce waste. The team agreed that a simple method to monitor demand versus capacity needed to be developed as part of the future state.

The team decided to address the needs of internal customers as part of the discussion of the following future state questions.

How Often Will We Check Performance?

Given that the expected lead time of the future state will be less than ninety days, and that a development project should be completed every two weeks (or ten working days), the VSM team decided that the appropriate frequency to review process performance and the status of projects is weekly, or every five days. For this weekly review, the team decided to create a visual board that displays the status of each project in process. The board will be worker managed, and will make use of "traffic light" techniques to quickly convey status. Key milestones in the development process will be defined, along with their expected completion dates, and posted on the board. An example of such a board is provided in Figure 8.1.

Green indicates that a milestone is on schedule to be met. Yellow indicates that a milestone is in danger of not being met and that corrective action may be necessary. Red indicates that a milestone will not be met and that corrective action will be required in order to get the project back on track. Team members will have the authority to change the status at any time, but not less frequently than weekly.

Project	Define Reqs	Develop Specs.	Design Proto.	Proto. Complete	Tooling Avail.	Prod. Verif.
ABC	COMP	9/1 ●	9/15 ●	9/22 ●	10/21	10/28
DEF	COMP	9/8 ○	9/22 ○	9/29 ○	10/28	11/05
GHI	COMP	COMP	COMP	COMP	9/20 ●	9/28

Figure 8.1   Visual status board.

The team also discussed the possibility of increasing the frequency of reviewing performance in the future, if they see a benefit to doing so. But for now, they believe that the weekly review will be sufficient to provide a beat, a pace, or a rhythm to the development process and improve its ability to meet the established service level. They also felt that the visual status board could be designed in such a way that it could be used as well as a capacity-planning tool to monitor demand versus capacity.

Lean Note

As noted in chapter 6, the frequency of review of performance has also been called "management timeframe" or "pitch." It is not uncommon for an organization or team to change the frequency of its review over time, once it has seen the benefits of frequent but simple reviews of performance. Often, teams will increase the frequency or pitch and will realize additional benefits by doing so.

Which Steps Create Value and Which Are Waste?

In reviewing the current state map, the most apparent waste is defects or correction. The first pass yield for the current development process is 8.1 percent. Further, the VSM team recognizes that there is nonvalue-added time embedded in the various estimated process times due to the presence of incomplete and inaccurate information.

For example, the team estimated that approximately 50%, or twenty hours, of the process time for the Develop Specifications step involves obtaining clarity on requirements, chasing after missing information from the previous step, and related activities. Therefore, the process time for Develop Specifications can be significantly reduced if the quality of information can be improved from 50 percent complete and accurate to, say 95 percent, in the future state. A similar discussion of subsequent process steps resulted in estimated reductions in process time of approximately sixteen hours for Design Prototype, and eight hours for Create Final Drawings." Although it is difficult to precisely estimate the new process times, the team was confident that these reductions could be achieved in the future state by improving the information quality to a level of 95 percent in each of the initial processes. These changes were noted on the current state map (Figure 8.2).

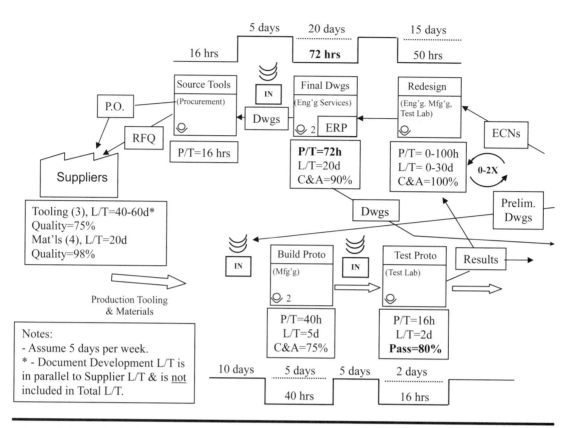

Figure 8.2 **"Marked up" current state map (with changes in bold).**

To improve the information quality, the team identified the need for a comprehensive voice-of-the-customer checklist to be used at the very first process step, Define Requirements. This checklist will include information needed by *all* subsequent processes and functions. In addition, the VSM team decided that it would be better to involve Manufacturing Engineering during the Define Requirements process, rather than later in the process when preliminary drawings were created, as occurs in the current state. Although this would result in additional process time at this step—an estimated additional eight hours—the team believed that the output of this important step would be significantly improved as a result. During the discussion, the team agreed that involving Manufacturing Engineering at this step would have no lead time impact.

The team also identified nonvalue-added processing waste within the Design Prototype process. This was associated with the reuse of existing design elements or, more specifically, the difficulty in doing so. The team believed that an approximate 25 percent reduction in process time, or a reduction of twenty hours, could be realized by the implementation of a design library with quick look-up capability. In addition, the team decided that specific manufacturing standards should be identified and considered during the Design Prototype process. These ideas will provide benefits in subsequent process steps, such

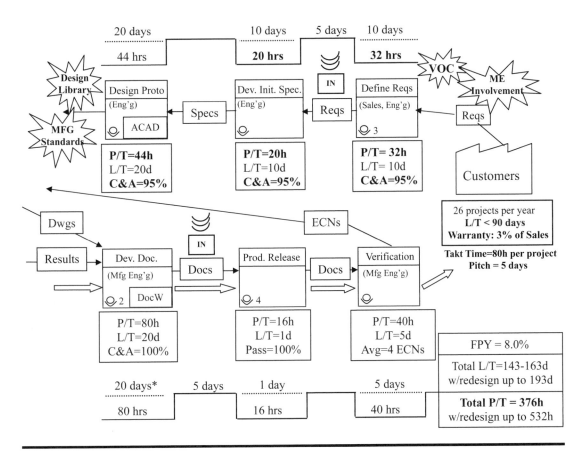

Figure 8.2 *(Continued)*

as during prototype testing. Certainly the pass rate would increase as existing design elements are used more often, and as designs adhere more to established manufacturing standards. The team estimated that the new pass rate would be 80 percent, as shown in Figure 8.2.

The team identified a significant waiting waste at various points in the current state—an estimated twenty-five days in queues prior to particular process steps. In addition, the Tooling Supplier lead time of forty to sixty days represented major waiting waste. The team decided to address these stoppages in flow during discussion of the next future state question.

How Can We Flow Work with Fewer Interruptions?

The main cause for the queue prior to Develop Specifications was attributed to the fact that the engineer who was involved in the Define Requirements step was not the same engineer who would develop the specifications. In the future state, the VSM team decided that this would always be the same person. Therefore, this queue or interruption could be eliminated. Further, the team believed that the Develop Specifications step could be rolled into the Define Requirements step, performing them more concurrently. The team challenged itself to complete these two steps within ten days, as noted in Figure 8.3.

The queues prior to build Prototype and Test Prototype were attributed to the fact that the resources required at these steps were "shared" resources. In other words, they had other responsibilities, specifically to support Production, which always had priority.

The team assessed that, with an acceptable investment, build and test capability could be provided within six months for sole use by Development personnel. This would effectively eliminate these potential interruptions in flow, thereby saving approximately fifteen days in lead time.

Building on the cross-functional approach taken at the Define Requirements/Develop Specifications steps, the VSM team also decided that maintaining a cross-functional team approach would help improve flow throughout the design process. This team would include an engineer, a Manufacturing engineer, and an Engineering service person, as well as a Production associate who would help to build prototypes. This would prevent any resource conflicts from arising, provide

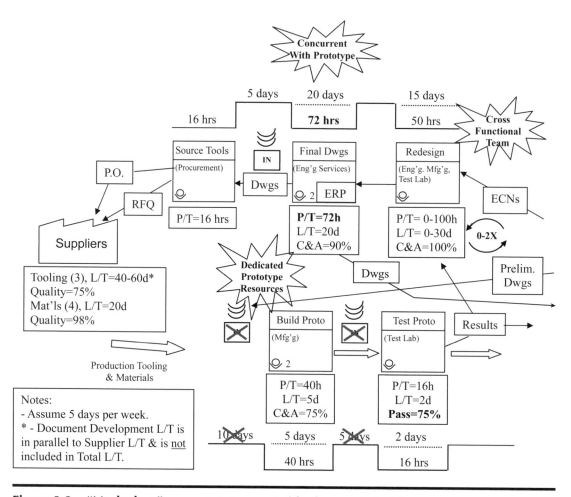

Figure 8.3 "Marked up" current state map (with changes in bold).

a sense of team throughout the development process, and allow for Engineering documentation (e.g., drawings) to be completed concurrently with the prototype design, build, and test process. In addition, with the team concept envisioned, the Production Release step can be rolled into the Verification process, thereby eliminating the five-day queue prior to Production Release. Given the volume of development projects each year, the VSM team thought that this was a reasonable approach.

With the reductions in process time identified so far, and disregarding the Procurement- and Sales-related activities, the estimated process time for the team's remaining activities is approximately 352 hours. Therefore, an estimated 4.4 people would be required (352 hours ÷ 80 hours = 4.4). The team felt that additional gains would be realized once implemented, and decided that they would begin with a four-person team representing the functions previously mentioned. Adjustments in the size of the team can be made after the future state has been implemented and the team has gained sufficient experience in the new development process.

The VSM team estimated the new lead time from Specification to Final Drawings to be twenty days—a significant reduction from the current forty-seven days, excluding queue time, which, as mentioned previously, will be eliminated.

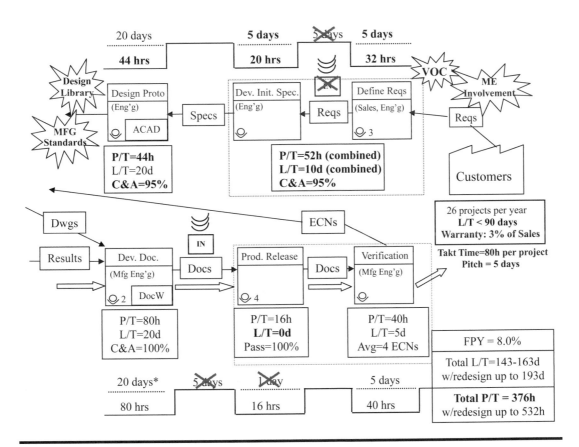

Figure 8.3 *(Continued)*

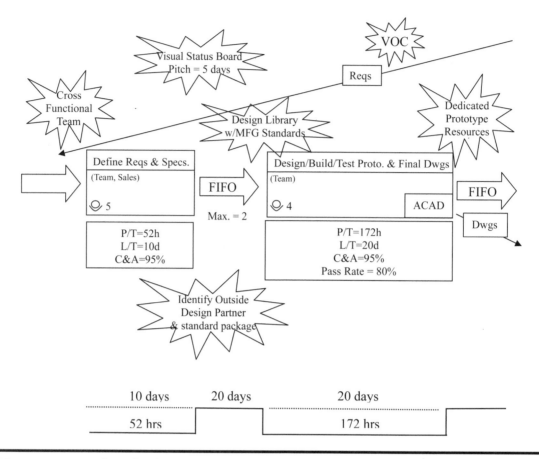

Figure 8.4   DevelopTek's future state map.

At this time, the VSM team felt prepared to visually depict the future state that they were envisioning (see Figure 8.4A/B).

Mapping Tip

It is very common for mapping teams to begin to create the actual future state map at this point in the process. Mapping teams should begin by marking up the current state map during discussion of the first four future state questions, and *then* begin to draw the future state map. When mapping teams attempt to create the future state map too soon, there is a tendency for them to get caught up in the mechanics of creating the map and not have sufficient discussion of the future state questions.

The remaining interruption that must be addressed involves the order and receipt of tooling and materials. The VSM team contacted the key tooling suppliers to gain a better understanding of their process. They quickly discovered that twenty days of the forty- to sixty-day lead time involved the ordering of raw material from which the tooling would be fabricated. The VSM team decided that the company would purchase the tool steel itself early in the process, and have

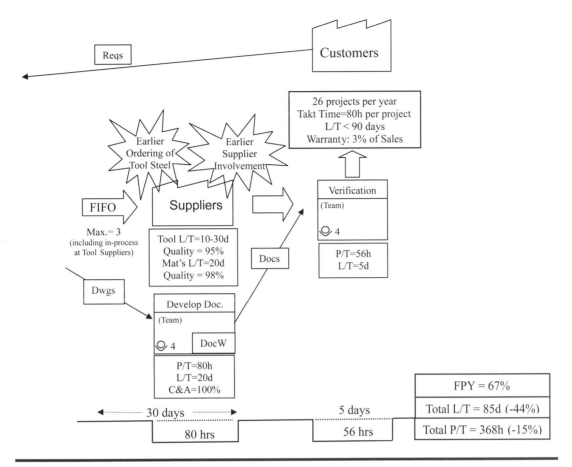

Figure 8.4 *(Continued)*.

it sent to the tool supplier at the appropriate time. This would effectively reduce tooling lead time by twenty days.

In addition, the team decided that earlier supplier involvement would provide other important benefits. A supplier "partner" would be selected early in the process, and that supplier would be asked to participate in the prototype design activity. The tooling suppliers estimated an additional ten-day reduction in lead time if they were involved sooner in the process, as well as improved quality, say 95 percent. Therefore, the expected tooling lead time for the future state would be ten to thirty days from availability of final drawings, a significant reduction from the current forty to sixty days, but still an interruption that must be managed. This will be addressed in the next future state question.

How Do We Control Work between Interruptions? How Will Work Be Prioritized?

The VSM team has designed a future state that will provide excellent flow throughout the front end of the process. However, there is still a possible interruption toward the beginning of the development process. This can result when the incoming demand of projects exceeds the development team's capacity to begin processing them in a timely manner. First, the team had to decide where best to locate a queue that could be closely monitored to identify when demand exceeds capacity. The team decided that it would be best located *after* the Define Requirements/Develop Specifications step and prior to Design/Build/Test Prototype step. Next, the team needed to establish a rule to prioritize this queue of work in the event that more than one project was available for the team to choose from to initiate the prototype activity. They agreed that, given the market sensitivity to lead time, the best approach was to work on development projects on a first-in-first-out (FIFO) basis. A limit on the size of this queue must also be established. Given the projected lead time for the new development process of sixty-five days (assuming a worst case of thirty days for the Tool Suppliers), well within the ninety-day goal, some queue is acceptable. Using the following calculation, the team determined that a maximum of two projects would be permitted at any given time:

Queue in terms of time = Lead time to Customer – Expected process lead time

= 90 days – 65 days = 25 days

With a Takt time of 10 days per project:

25 days ÷ 10 days per project = 2.5 projects, rounding down to 2 projects

In other words, if the queue toward the beginning of the development process grows to three projects or more, the process will be in jeopardy of meeting the overall lead time goal of ninety days because demand will exceed capacity at this time. In the unlikely case that this queue grows to three projects, the team decided that it would then need to "pull" additional resources in the form of an external design firm that could Design/Build/Test Prototypes. The team decided to identify a design firm partner, create a standard design package, and provide training to the partners so that they would be prepared in case the need for additional resources arose. This practice would allow for the internal cross-functional development team to take corrective action to recover if problems arose with any particular project during the Design/Build/Test Prototype step.

There is also the interruption within the development process as the team waits for tools and materials to arrive so that the Verification process can be performed—an expected ten- to thirty-day wait time. Development of production documentation will be completed during this time. Still, the interruption in flow can allow for specific problems to arise. There can be the opportunity to revert to "push," during which too many projects can find their way into the development process at one time, resulting in extended lead times. There is also the possibility that the desired sequence of jobs could be lost. Still another problem is that the flow of projects to the Verification process may be disrupted. This could happen if a major redesign effort is required or an unexpected problem arises at the tool supplier.

It is highly desirable to be able to minimize the impact on the overall flow of the process when such problems arise. A means to buffer for such issues and to have a process for recovering must be a part of the future state. The VSM team depicted this queue on the future state map, along with the rules in terms of desired sequence (FIFO), and the number of projects allowed, including those in process at the tooling supplier (a maximum of three). The team determined the maximum number of projects allowable at this point in the process by the following calculation:

Tooling supplier lead time = 10 to 30 days, assuming worse case = 30 days

With a Takt time of 10 days per project:

30 days ÷ 10 days per project = 3 projects

With three projects in queue and/or in process at the tooling suppliers at any time, uninterrupted flow through this important step and beyond can be better ensured, *without* increasing development process lead time beyond what is acceptable. It would also allow time for some corrective action to be taken in case a problem arises with a particular project at the tooling supplier. Even with this standard level of work-in-process, the total lead time for the development process is projected to be eighty-five days, still within the ninety-day goal.

By adhering to the rules to be established for the two key queues in the development process, the amount of projects in process at any time is controlled, thereby maintaining a more predictable overall lead time. By maintaining visibility and attention to these queues, decisions can be made in a timely manner that will maintain flow through the development process and a predictable lead time. Further, the envisioned process will allow for development resources to effectively respond to potential problems, without the need for excessive expediting to maintain flow. Such expediting often is done at the expense of quality.

How Can We Level the Volume of Work and the Mix of Activities?

The queue after the Define Requirements/Develop Specifications step will allow for action to be taken in the case that the volume of work (i.e., demand) varies to the point that it impacts the flow of development projects through the envisioned system. The complexity of projects does not vary significantly enough to warrant enhancement of the rules for processing beyond FIFO. If a difficult development project is encountered, sufficient flexibility has been included in the envisioned development process to respond accordingly. Therefore, no further changes to the future state will be required.

What Process Improvements Will Be Necessary?

The team listed all of the process improvements identified during discussion of the first six future state questions—the various kaizen bursts on the future state map. From these kaizen bursts, an implementation plan will be developed to achieve the future state over the coming months. The team will clarify each kaizen and identify the specific steps necessary to complete each. The team will also identify individual responsibility for following through on each kaizen, along with an expected date of completion. The resources required will be determined, expected benefits estimated, and priorities made accordingly.

The team estimated the new value stream summary measures for the future state. The total lead time is projected to be 85 days, representing a 44 percent reduction from the average current state lead time of 153 days (not including redesign). The total process time is estimated to be approximately 368 hours, including 8 hours of Procurement time per project that is *not* depicted on the future state map. This represents an approximate 15% reduction in process time. Finally, the team estimates that the new first pass yield will be 67 percent, close to its initial goal of 70 percent. However, the feeling of the team was that the reduction in process time and the improvement in first pass yield would be greater than currently projected. All agreed that these will be key performance measures for the new development process that will be tracked to assess the impact of the new system and the associated tools and techniques that will be implemented in the future state.

In the final chapter of the book, we will explore the implementation strategies necessary to achieve the future state.

Chapter 9

Achieving the Future State

General Guidelines

Although it is impossible to describe an implementation strategy that fits all possible situations, there are some general guidelines to consider. Typically, the initial focus of the future state implementation is on the waste that most significantly affects the current state of most development processes: defect and correction waste. The quality of information as measured by "percent complete and accurate" and "first pass yield" must be addressed first. It will be nearly impossible to improve flow through the development process without improving information quality. Furthermore, by reducing this waste, valuable capacity will be freed up to allow work on other process improvements identified during the future state design.

Means to improve information quality are most often inexpensive to implement and can have a significant impact in a relatively short time, usually within three months. Well-designed checklists can be developed and implemented quickly and, usually, fairly easily. Improving the processes used to obtain the "voice-of-the-customer" is part of this initial effort. Whether by use of simple checklists, or more advanced concepts, accurate voice-of-the-customer information is essential to the success of the development process. Often, additional lead time is required to ensure that correct information is obtained. This initial investment in lead time will often result in less required process and lead time later in the development process.

Based on the nature of the development process and the business itself, another early effort may be to reassess the development projects currently in progress or being considered. There are a number of effective techniques that we can quickly implement to address project selection methods that are lacking or are incomplete. Market assessment tools, financial models, and the like can be used for such purposes, and implemented within three months. The result may be the cancellation or postponement of particular projects as their importance to the business is reconsidered. Although this may have a negative impact on morale within the development process, particularly for the people who were involved in projects that were cancelled or postponed, the result will be to free up resources that can be directed to more important projects, and to the future state implementation effort. In other words, nonvalue-added processing waste can be removed from the current process by cancelling or avoiding projects that will not result in significant value creation for the business.

The team may also determine that particular projects can be postponed in order to reduce the number of projects in progress. This can provide quick benefits to the organization (again, within three months), as development resources can focus on fewer projects. However, the transition from a "push" system with many projects in process to a leveled "pull" system can be difficult. Although this requires little or no investment, management will need to make and adhere to difficult decisions regarding priorities. It almost requires a "leap of faith" from management to believe that flow and throughput will increase, while the amount of work-in-process decreases.

As you can see, the initial focus is to reduce waste within the development process in order to free up valuable and limited resources. You can also see that the most common approach to the application of Lean thinking to the development process is to start at the beginning of the development process—the point closest to the customer. Another common strategy is to initially implement techniques that do not require a major investment in computer-based information technology tools. In most organizations, such tools can take twelve to twenty-four months to successfully implement. An organization cannot wait this long to see benefits.

Once waste has been reduced within the process, the focus usually moves to improving the process of reusing existing knowledge. Improving the efficiency and effectiveness of knowledge reuse can often require a considerable investment of time and effort, though not always in information technology. Developing design standards, including manufacturing standards, usually requires the involvement of key personnel within the organization. The team must resolve differences between historic approaches, and must agree on standards. This is not an easy thing to accomplish. It takes willingness and persistence, but it can be done.

Next, this existing knowledge must be captured in a format that is easily accessible. Design standards can quickly be documented in the form of checklists, templates, and/or guidelines that can be used on new designs. The difficulty usually is in taking existing designs and identifying the principle standards on which they were designed as well as their performance characteristics. The team will need to define these principles and characteristics and develop a database that makes the information easy to access. While setting up a database is not difficult these days, given the availability of various database development tools, the real effort is in obtaining the information necessary for the database. It can take three to six months to implement effective tools to improve the knowledge reuse process. However, an organization can realize benefits quickly upon the tools' implementation. By implementing concepts that improve standard work practices throughout the development process, organizations can reduce additional nonvalue-added processing waste.

Once organizations have reduced waste and improved the quality of information, their focus must turn to improving flow. Of course, flow will improve as information quality improves. However, let's say that an organization has decided to take an approach that involves the implementation of cross-functional, co-located teams. These organizations can expect that it will take three to six months (and sometimes longer) to implement such teams. Although physical co-location can be accomplished relatively quickly (within three months), additional time is necessary for the members to fully develop into a high-performing team. Members must develop required team-building skills, define roles and ground rules, receive technical training and cross-training, and establish performance measures. Also, difficult interpersonal issues (e.g., conflicts) can arise. Because of this, the team's make-up must be carefully considered. Changes in team membership may be necessary if the team experiences significant difficulties over time. Close facilitation is often required to overcome these issues.

Lean Note

It is imperative that an organization possess the requisite technical knowledge for the industry or industries in which it operates. Collectively, the development resources within the organization must possess sufficient technical knowledge and skills in order to succeed over time. It is possible that an organization does not have the skilled and experienced resources that it needs to succeed. This is not a negative reflection on the individual resources, but rather on the organization as a whole for not providing adequate personal development opportunities to these resources. In recent years, many organizations have made cuts in personnel development programs. These include, but are not limited to: technical education programs, programs that involve rotation of technical assignments, cross-training, and even attendance at trade shows. For organizations that have not focused on this kind of development, it must become an urgent priority in the future state implementation. It may take quite some time to develop internal resources or to identify and obtain external resources. Today, more than ever, organizations must invest in the development of their technical resources if they hope to succeed in the long run.

Once flow is improved, the team will then typically focus on continuing to improve efficiency. The expanded use of existing development tools or the implementation of new development tools can often take six to twelve months to complete before the organization begins to see the benefits. Training programs must be developed and implemented, and information system changes and the like completed.

Developing an Implementation Plan

To develop a reasonable implementation plan for the significant undertaking required to successfully implement the future state, organizations should identify several "loops" on the future state map. Loops are typically pockets of flow within the new development system defined on the future state map (Figure 9.1A/B). There are no set rules to identify loops. They tend to be portions of the future state that the team feels they can "get their hands around" with regard to implementation. Loops, and the kaizens within each, can then be prioritized.

It is important to prioritize the kaizens to develop an achievable plan over time. For the DevelopTek case study, we might identify three loops:(1) a Learning loop that includes developing requirements and specifications, along with prototyping; (2) a Supplier loop; and (3) an Execution loop (see Figure 9.1A/B) that includes developing documentation and verification.

The team's next step is to prioritize the loops, probably starting with the Learning loop for reasons previously discussed in this chapter, and the individual kaizens within. The team will next identify a detailed implementation plan for each kaizen. This requires the value stream mapping (VSM) team to think through each kaizen and what will be involved. This process includes identifying

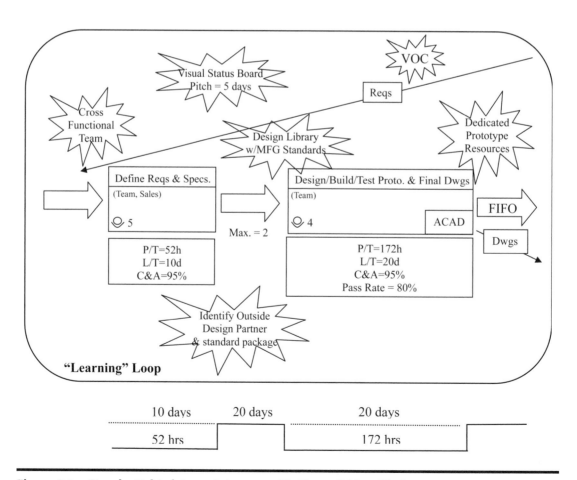

Figure 9.1 DevelopTek's future state map with "loops" identified.

Achieving the Future State ■ 93

a responsible person to head up each kaizen, along with expected completion dates, and an assessment of the resources required.

We created a simplified implementation plan for DevelopTek as an example (Figure 9.2).

A quick review of the plan shows that the majority of the future state will be implemented within nine months, leaving only the work involving the outside design partner to be completed within an additional three months. Of course, this is just one possible example of an Implementation Plan.

Concluding the Mapping Event

Value stream mapping events are learning opportunities. Any team that goes through this process will learn a great deal about their existing process, and the means to improve it. Other staff within the organization will want to know what happened during the event and what decisions have been made regarding the future state. Organizations will need to communicate this vision for the future, as well as the plan to get there, to all staff.

At the conclusion of every VSM event, the team should "report out" to other members in the organization. Report outs provide a means to extend the learning across the organization. In large organizations, a series of report outs

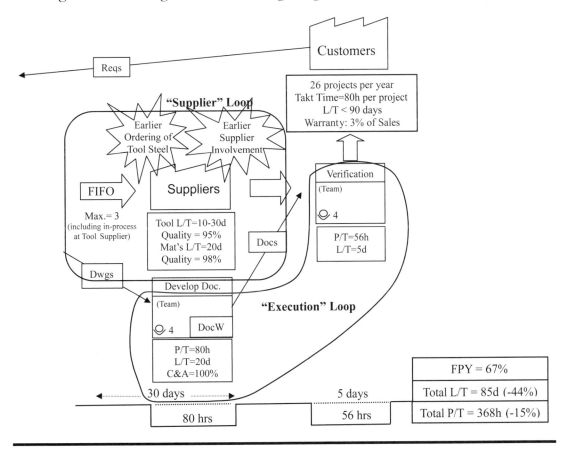

Figure 9.1 *(Continued)*

may be scheduled shortly upon completion of the event. The team will make use of the documentation developed during the event as a reference for these report outs. The documentation includes the SIPOC (supplier–input–process–output–customer), the current state map, current state reflections, the future state map along with projected benefits, and the implementation plan. The documentation provides an excellent means to effectively communicate this important information.

The documentation must be kept up to date as progress is made on the future state implementation. The value stream map, as well as the value stream measures, should be updated as changes are made. Maintaining the implementation plan, as well as the maps, usually is the responsibility of the value stream manager.

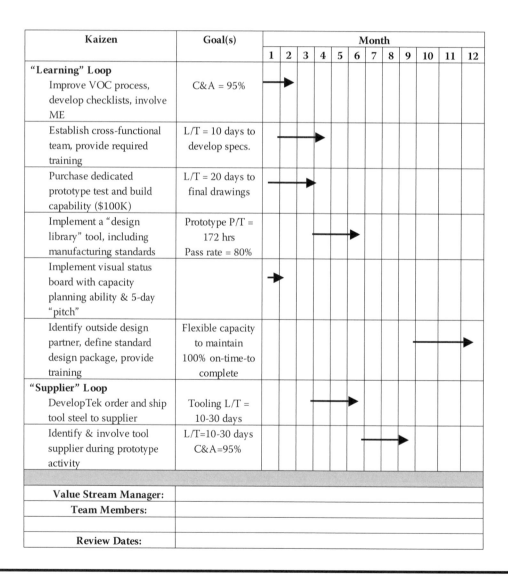

Kaizen	Goal(s)	Month											
		1	2	3	4	5	6	7	8	9	10	11	12
"Learning" Loop Improve VOC process, develop checklists, involve ME	C&A = 95%	→											
Establish cross-functional team, provide required training	L/T = 10 days to develop specs.	→											
Purchase dedicated prototype test and build capability ($100K)	L/T = 20 days to final drawings	→											
Implement a "design library" tool, including manufacturing standards	Prototype P/T = 172 hrs Pass rate = 80%				→								
Implement visual status board with capacity planning ability & 5-day "pitch"		→											
Identify outside design partner, define standard design package, provide training	Flexible capacity to maintain 100% on-time-to complete										→		
"Supplier" Loop DevelopTek order and ship tool steel to supplier	Tooling L/T = 10-30 days				→								
Identify & involve tool supplier during prototype activity	L/T=10-30 days C&A=95%						→						
Value Stream Manager:													
Team Members:													
Review Dates:													

Figure 9.2   DevelopTek implementation plan.

Posting this information visibly, in prominent areas of the organization, is also recommended. This practice will better ensure that the documentation is kept up to date. Keeping the information locked away in a file cabinet typically does not work well.

Enabling Value Stream Management

The difficult task of successfully implementing the future state will fall to a large degree on the value stream manager and the VSM team. However, they will need the support of other members in the organization. The Steering Committee, Lead Team, or Decision Panel—whatever term you wish to use—must fully support the effort over time. Typically, these groups represent senior managers. Their role is to help the team address political, technical, and other obstacles that might be encountered during the implementation of the future state. Periodic reviews with the VSM team should be scheduled. Remember that the development process is one of the three key value streams within the enterprise. Change will not come easily, but the rewards for the organization can be great.

The value stream manager is usually the person who has the greatest stake in the development process—the vice president of Development, the manager of Engineering—whatever title he or she may hold. This is not a role that can be delegated. The person fulfilling this role should have strong project management skills (e.g., organization, planning, communication). These skills can be applied to the management of the implementation process.

The value stream manager will need strong interpersonal skills because conflict is sure to arise. Most often, the changes represented in the future state have broad cross-functional ramifications. Disagreements are sure to arise and must be effectively overcome. Also, team members *must* continue to support the effort well beyond the mapping event. Therefore, strong and persistent leadership will be required.

An effective set of process performance measures will need to be implemented as part of the future state. The value stream manager must drive the implementation and upkeep of these measures. Potential measures for consideration include:

- Average Lead time per project (to monitor performance to the service levels established)
- Development cost per project (including process time)
- First pass yield or some other measure of "internal" quality performance
- Customer satisfaction (a measure of value—did the customer or market accept the product or service at the expected price)

Other measures used by organizations that have successfully "Leaned" their development process include:

- Percent on time–complete (to established due dates).
- Percent within target cost (an important performance measure that monitors the quality of the early decision-making process within the development system).
- Projects in process (to monitor adherence to established pull system rules).
- Percentage reuse (where higher is better to encourage reuse).

What happens beyond the implementation of the first future state? Who will have responsibility for the continuous improvement of the development process? If an organization is really going to practice Lean thinking, it must continually challenge itself to improve. Will it be the value stream manager? If so, his or her role and responsibilities will go well beyond that described here with regard to the implementation of the first future state.

In the end, this workbook provides a methodology for applying Lean thinking to the development process. We hope that it has provided the reader with enough information, guidelines, and examples to successfully accomplish this important task. However, the methodology is simply a "means" to meet an objective. There is more to Lean thinking than methodologies. By this point, the reader should have an appreciation that Lean requires a different way of thinking, acting, interacting, communicating, and making decisions. Eighty percent of Lean is behavioral. The key to success is to change people's behaviors—the very culture of the organization. If the organization is truly committed to the Lean path, a sincere discussion of what this really means must take place. Only then will an organization realize the full benefits of Lean.

APPENDIX

Target Costing and Cost Modeling

Target costing is a very basic concept that can be very powerful if properly used. It is calculated as:

$$\text{Target cost} = \text{Projected price} - \text{Desired margin}$$

Many companies spend a lot of time and effort to estimate the cost of new products and services. They then add a margin to the cost estimate in order to establish a price for the product or service that they offer to the market. It is more effective for a company to continually study its market and competition in order to understand the price or prices that a market will bear. Since companies cannot typically control the market price and know what is and is not an acceptable margin, their focus must move to the target cost and the key drivers of cost. If the target cost cannot be met, the project should be cancelled; it's that simple. Therefore, target costing can be *one* tool to determine which design projects should be cancelled and which should be pursued.

The target cost should be calculated at the beginning of a project and then compared to estimated costs throughout the development process to ensure that the resulting margin is acceptable to the company before the product is in production. To do this, organizations must develop a cost model that clearly depicts the key drivers of cost. Such a tool allows the design effort to be prioritized, focusing on the key drivers of cost and appropriate "trade-off" decisions to be made.

There are five key elements of cost that should be included in the cost model and that can be affected by design. These elements, as well as some opportunities to be considered in the design, are listed below. Note that there can be strong overlapping of some.

Cost Element	Design Opportunities
Direct labor	■ Simplify assembly ■ Automation (which can add to capital equipment and indirect overhead costs) ■ Reduce quality assurance (test, inspection) time
Direct material	■ Use of readily available and typically lower cost materials ■ Decrease possibility for scrap or waste generated in the process
Design cost	■ Use existing in-house design elements ■ Use commercially available components ■ Improve the effectiveness and efficiency of design
Indirect overhead	■ Reduce material handling and storage requirements ■ Reduce need to changeover or set-up equipment ■ Use existing parts, reduce number of parts that must be purchased, stored, and controlled
Capital equipment	■ Use existing equipment, tooling, and processes ■ Open up tolerances where possible to allow use of existing equipment

The following template can be used to identify various product cost drivers. It is not meant to be complete. Rather, the template is intended to encourage organizations to consider various aspects of cost that they may have overlooked in past design efforts. Further, it can be used to prioritize the design effort from a cost standpoint, and to compare various design options under consideration.

Cost Driver	Estimate
Direct Labor	
■ Time of assemblers, machine operators, etc.	
■ Time of quality assurance personnel (inspection, test)	
■ Other	
Direct Material – Consider full acquisition cost	
■ Purchase price of all materials use	
■ Scrap and/or waste	
■ Transportation	
■ Initial stocking costs	
■ Inventory carrying cost	
■ Possible obsolescence	
■ Other	

Cost Driver	Estimate
Design Cost	
■ Time of design engineers and support personnel	
■ Time of operations, test, and other personnel involved	
■ Use of outside services (e.g., design, test)	
■ Design support during introduction and beyond	
■ Other	
Indirect Cost	
■ Utilities	
■ Material storage and handling	
■ Transportation	
■ Warranty	
■ Ongoing support personnel (e.g., cost accounting, process engineering, supervision, and management)	
■ Training (start-up and ongoing)	
■ Sales and marketing	
■ Other	
Capital Equipment	
■ New equipment purchases	
■ Tooling	
■ Facility changes	
■ Other	

Quality Function Deployment

Quality function deployment (QFD) is a methodology used to capture the "voice of the customer" and translate customer needs into design requirements and specifications. It was initially developed at Mitsubishi's Kobe, Japan, shipyards in 1972, and adopted by Toyota in the late 1970s. Mitsubishi and Toyota's results (60 percent reductions in design costs and 40 percent reduction in design time) captured the attention of organizations in the United States, and, by 1986, Ford, Xerox, GE, and other companies had adopted the model. When used properly, it is a powerful tool to ensure that a complete and accurate understanding of customer needs exists at the earliest stages of the development process (Juran, 1993, King, 1989).

It also allows for customer-driven prioritization and trade-offs to be performed in the design process across the various product functions and

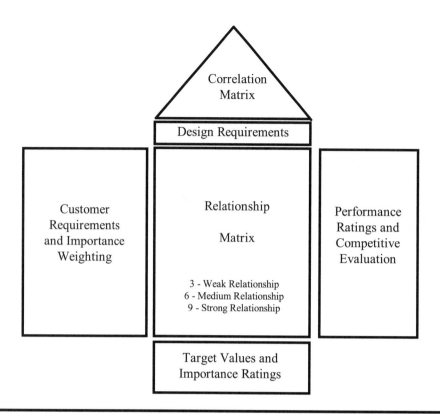

Figure A.1   House of Quality: general format.

requirements. The methodology relies strongly on what has been often called the "House of Quality" (Figure A.1). The House of Quality can convey a great deal of information regarding customer needs and design requirements, even depicting important interactions between them. Weighting techniques can help to identify priorities and assist in trade-off decision-making (Figure A.1 and Figure A.2).

Some companies have expanded the use of QFD to include processes as well as product development. Therefore, QFD becomes a technique consisting of a series of interlocking matrices that translate customer needs into product *and* process characteristics. This is displayed in Figure A.3 (Juran and Gryna, 1993).

Customer Requirements	Importance to customer (3 – high 1 – low)	Product Features (Relationship weights 3 (low) – 6 (medium) – 9 (high))						Competitive Evaluation (5 - best)		
		Paper width	Paper Thickness	Roll Roundness	Coating Thickness	Tensile Strength	Paper Color	Us	A	B
Paper will not tear	3	3	6	9		9		1	3	3
Consistent finish	1				6			3	2	4
No ink bleed	2		9		6			5	4	3
Prints cleanly	3			6	9		6			
Importance Weighting		9	36	45	45	27	18			
Target Values		x-mm	t-mm	r-mm	c-microns	5 lbs	y-std			
Technical Evaluation		Us:5 A:5 B:4	Us:3 A:4 B:2	Us:2 A:4 B:5	Us:3 A:4 B:2	Us:3 A:4 B:4	Us:4 A:3 B:3			

Figure A.2   House of Quality: paper example.

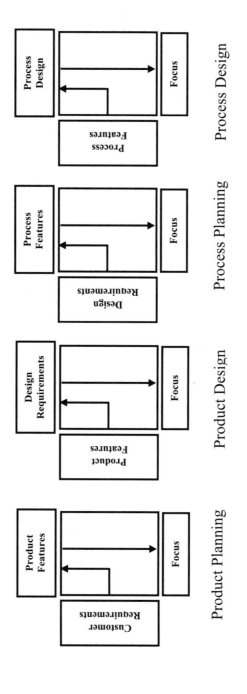

Figure A.3   QFD used throughout product and process development.

Pugh Matrix

A Pugh Matrix, also known as a "criteria-based matrix," is used to compare several different design concepts being considered. These matrices allow the user to compare the different concepts, create strong alternative concepts from weaker concepts, and arrive at the "optimal" concept, which may be a combination or variant of the best aspects of the other concepts. The tool does not require much quantitative data. Comparisons are typically done qualitatively [plus (+), minus (-), same (S)]. Simple addition of +s and -s provides the analysis "score."

To use a Pugh Matrix, companies must first identify a "base" or "reference" concept against which other ideas will be compared. This is typically the concept that the team feels most strongly about at a particular point in the design process. It is usually the best current concept under consideration at a particular time.

To adequately use the Pugh Matrix, the team must input the critical-to-success factors identified from a "voice of the customer" (VOC) exercise (e.g., focus groups, surveys). The basic template of the matrix follows.

Critical to Success Factors (Derived from VOC data)	Importance (From VOC data)	Reference Concept	Concept #2	Concept 3#
1.		Datum		
2.				
3.				
4.				
# of Minus (–)				
# of Plus (+)				
# of Same (S)				
	Analysis "Score" =			

A completed example is provided below. This example shows that the Reference Concept is still the best alternative (Concepts #2 and #3 both have negative scores), but that it may be possible to incorporate positive attributes from the other concepts into the Reference.

One approach is to "weight" the pluses (+) and minuses (–) by the importance ratings for the critical success factors; another is to incorporate them into the House of Quality.

Critical to Success Factors (Derived from VOC data)	Importance (From VOC data)	Reference Concept	Concept #2	Concept #3
1. Reliable	54	Datum	–	–
2. Safe operation	52		–	–
3. Price	48		S	S
4. Appearance	30		+	S
# of Minus (–)			2	2
# of Plus (+)			1	0
# of Same (S)			1	2
	Analysis "Score" =		–1	–2

Set-Based Concurrent Engineering (SBCE)

The term *set-based concurrent engineering* was coined by Allen Ward and his colleagues at the University of Michigan as they studied Toyota's product design process in the mid-1990s. They observed that Toyota practiced a form of concurrent engineering that was quite different from other companies. The Product Development teams are not always co-located. Personnel, with the exception of the chief engineer and staff, are not always dedicated to particular vehicle programs.

Nevertheless, Toyota's design participants still practice concurrent engineering by reasoning, developing, and communicating about sets of solutions in parallel and relatively independently. As the various designs under consideration are developed, they are "narrowed" as more information from development, testing, the customer, and across the organization itself is obtained.

Conversely, most other companies quickly decide on a single solution, attempting to avoid wasting limited resources on solutions that will ultimately not be used. However, with these practices, wastes typically appear much later in the design process when solutions well into their development phase (even in production) have to be changed. The cost of design changes tends to increase through the development process. This has been referred to as the "rule of tens"—the cost of a design change increases tenfold with each phase of design (e.g., concept to design to validation to production).

Therefore, it is worthwhile to adequately invest in the early stages of design by considering multiple alternatives in parallel. Though it may be true that the lead time of the early design stages may increase, there will be a reduction in overall design lead time. Further, potential lead time increases may be mitigated by using rapid learning cycles, rapid prototype techniques, effective and efficient communication of knowledge, cross-functional involvement to identify design for manufacturability issues early in the process, etc.

The key principles have been summarized by Ward, et al. as:

- Focus on system design
- The effective and efficient creating, dissemination, and use of knowledge
- Working with multiple alternative designs (i.e., "sets") simultaneously

These key principles are sometimes overlooked by companies attempting to use other design-related tools. For example, the Pugh matrix seeks to achieve a controlled convergence of alternative concepts, much like SBCE. However, the means of sharing the information between engineers working on different alternatives (the second principle listed above) is often left unaddressed.

Toyota has engineering checklists that are used to ensure the effective and efficient communication of information between engineers working on different alternatives. These checklists prompt discussion of design possibilities, given cost, and capability limitations, as opposed to the "best solution at the time." Although this appears to be a subtle distinction, it is critically important to the Toyota design process. A key benefit of SBCE is the possibility of a collaborative design that takes the best attributes from the different alternatives. Ward et al. termed these "intersections." Collaboration also refers to how the different design teams work together at points in the process, as opposed to the traditional competitive nature between teams. It is not important which design (and team) won, but that the best design was created.

Ward et al. (1996) further defined the principles of SBCE as:

- Define the feasible regions.
- Communicate the sets of possibilities.
- Look for "intersections."
- Explore trade-offs by designing multiple alternatives.
- Impose minimum constraint.
- Narrow sets smoothly, balancing the need to learn and the need to decide.
- Pursue high risk and conservative options in parallel.
- Establish feasibility before commitment.
- Stay within sets once committed.
- Control by managing uncertainty at process gates.
- Seek solutions robust to physical, market, and design variation.

3P and Concurrent Engineering

One process that has garnered a lot of attention in recent years is "3P" (Production Preparation Process). In 3P, product development and manufacturing process design are merged, thereby achieving the objective of concurrent engineering, which is to design the product and process simultaneously. This process can be used for a new product, a design change to an existing product, or a change in the demand for a product.

3P was developed by Chichiro Nakao, who worked for a Japanese consulting firm. Although 3P is not a Toyota-developed term, Toyota uses these underlying concepts, particularly the cross-functional approach to product design and the trying out of various design alternatives. It is a disciplined, methodical procedure to facilitate the rapid evaluation of ideas for product design and production processes. The product also is designed concurrently or in conjunction with the production process (Figure A.4).

A major element of 3P is to design by rapid prototype. This involves hands-on experimentation, not just of the product design, but the means to manufacture it. This method has been called "trystorming." Instead of simply brainstorming (creating ideas), trystorming puts to test the ideas under consideration in order to more effectively assess them. For trystorming to work, effective and efficient means to assess ideas must be provided. This is sometimes referred to as "rapid prototyping." 3P allows organizations to try a solution, not just simply develop an engineering drawing. The key is to prototype not just the product, but also the manufacturing process.

Methods that allow for rapid prototyping can be as simple as manufacturing mock-ups of production equipment, or actual prototype shops with

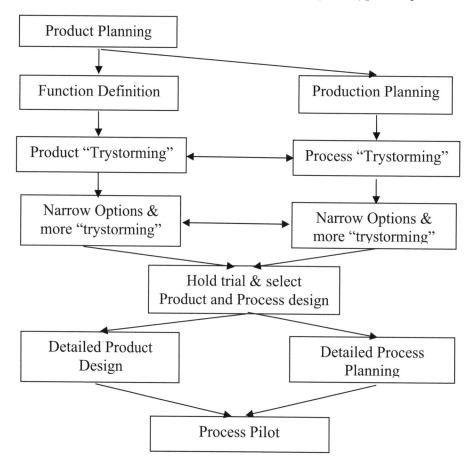

Figure A.4 Concurrent design process concept.

near-production or even production-like equipment available for experimentation. Techniques for developing product prototypes can be as simple as making models of the product using inexpensive and readily available materials, to stereo-lithography techniques that take mock-ups and make near-production ready samples.

The key is to focus on cross-functional involvement early in the product design process. Committing to manufacturing and purchasing or supplier involvement early in the design process allows for multiple perspectives and the generation of the best ideas. The other key is to encourage experimentation (trystorming) to assess ideas. It is strongly related to the concept frequently practiced at Toyota of going to the *gemba* (where the work is performed) for that is where the answers lie.

Design for Manufacturability (DFM)

Design for manufacturability (also referred to as design for manufacture and assembly—DFMA) centers around a group of common-sense concepts and techniques that ensure that a product design can be produced within projected cost. In this case, manufacturability refers to the company's ability to produce and test or inspect the product as well as its ability to purchase required materials. Therefore, supplier capability must also be a consideration. This process focuses on the reduction of manufacturing cost through decreasing labor and material costs. Specific techniques include reducing the total number of parts, the number of different parts, the total number of manufacturing operations, and making use of available production capabilities.

Of course, having a good understanding of the true needs of the customer is helpful, as consideration of manufacturing capabilities often turns to a discussion of trade-offs. Therefore, DFM is closely related to value engineering, which is a technique for evaluating the design of a product to assure that the essential functions are provided at a minimal overall cost to the manufacturer or user. In other words, don't provide "bells and whistles" when the customer doesn't *want* bells or whistles. The bells and whistles will certainly come at a cost. Therefore, a good question to ask is: "Can a design element be eliminated altogether?" Over-designing, in which the product performance exceeds the needs of the customer, also comes at a cost.

The specific techniques of DFM will vary based on the product being designed. Typically, ideas are generated as part of a brainstorming exercise involving cross-functional representatives to identify numerous alternatives to specific design elements being considered.

Some general questions to prompt meaningful discussion for mechanical design elements are

- Can a lesser level of quality be used? For example, can a coarser surface finish be used? Can a lesser flatness requirement be used?
- Can available or preexisting parts be used? Do design libraries exist where existing parts can be quickly identified for potential use?

- Can several parts be combined? What would be the impact on manufacturing? Consideration of size and weight must be given.
- What number and length of welds is really needed? Can welds be replaced by bends or mechanical fasteners? Less skilled labor would be required. What would be the impact on manufacturing?
- Can the type of fasteners be standardized? Can almost-like parts be made the same? Can the number of fasteners be reduced? Avoid two-part fasteners. Use captive or snap together fasteners where possible.
- Can the design be such that it allows for mistake-proofing techniques in assembly? Can parts be designed so that they can only be assembled or oriented in one way? Will the design lend itself to the use of fixtures in assembly?
- Can the parts be designed to be self-aligning or self-locating?
- How will part characteristics be assessed (e.g., inspected, tested)? Can they make use of available techniques?
- Are component dimensions compatible with the standard raw stock from which they will be made? Can the raw stock be easily purchased?
- What grade of material is really required? Can a lesser grade, alloy, etc., be used without jeopardizing design integrity?
- Will the materials being considered require any special handling or machining processes (e.g., hazardous materials)? What will be the impact on safety, cost?
- Can a casting be replaced with plastic components that can be molded, extruded, or formed? What would be the cost and lead time impact?
- What external processes will be required when internal capabilities do not exist? What will be the impact on cost and lead time?
- Can slots, pear-shaped holes, and other techniques be included in the design to permit use of less precise machining methods and to facilitate assembly?
- Can the design be modularized in a way that permits cellular manufacturing to be effectively used in production? Work balancing is a consideration here. Ideally, no module should require substantially more time than another.
- Can part accessibility and orientation be such that it allows for ease of manufacturing (e.g., top-down assembly)? Can the number of times a part has to be reoriented during assembly be reduced? How about the impact on machining? Will less complicated machining methods be required?
- What impact will the size and weight of components have on material handling in operations? Can less complicated methods be used?
- What is the labor required to prepare the finished product for transportation? Can the number of packaging components be reduced? Packaging is a design in and of itself. So, many of the questions previously stated will apply.

Some general questions and statements to prompt meaningful discussion for electrical design elements include:

- Can standard off-the-shelf electrical components be used? These typically require much less lead time to procure.

- Will the electrical components selected lend themselves to available manufacturing capability, such as surface mount or automated pick and place machines? Can secondary manual assembly be eliminated? Be certain to allow sufficient clearance for machine insertion.
- Align ICs (integrated circuits) and polarized components (e.g., diodes) in the same direction.
- Standardize hole sizes in through-hole boards.
- Can standard size circuit boards be used? What will be the impact on manufacturing of any "batching" of printed circuit boards where many smaller boards are made from a single larger board and then cut and/or trimmed?
- Can the number of layers of a printed circuit board be reduced, which typically results in lower cost?
- Would application-specific integrated circuits (ASICs) be less costly than a printed circuit board?
- Can the number of connections be reduced? Can standard connectors be used?
- Can software programming (e.g., burn-in, tuning) of components or the electrical assembly itself simplify the design and, in turn, the manufacturing process?
- What will be the impact on testing? Does the design lend itself to available testing capabilities? How about accessibility to perform required tests?
- What is the expected test cycle time? Can the test be modularized? What in-process testing can be performed to ensure product quality throughout the manufacturing process, rather than relying solely on an end-of-line test? Perhaps isolating design elements or partitioning techniques will allow for this.
- Does the printed circuit board or electronic assembly require a particular coating or epoxy potting? What is the cure time for coatings being considered? Can cure times be reduced with use of a specific coating or by use of elevated temperature cures?
- Do the materials being considered for use require any special handling or manufacturing processes? What impact will there be on safety, cost, waste disposal?

Some general questions to prompt meaningful discussion for software design elements include:

- Can software code be used from previous product designs? Can commercially available code be used?
- Can hardware functions be replaced with software?
- Can testing, adjustments, maintenance, etc. be handled by software?
- Are industry software development standards being used?
- Can user interface software or hardware be simplified?
- Are efficient software development tools being used to reduce development cost?
- How can the software be tested before being integrated with the hardware (e.g., simulations)? How can the code be easily debugged and corrected when problems arise?

■ How can upgrades be performed easily? Will modularity in software code make upgrades easier and less costly?

■ Are built-in-test or built-in-diagnostic capabilities warranted in the design?

A review of the questions presented reveals that the subject of DFM or DFMA really goes well beyond manufacturing. It also includes testability, reliability, maintainability, safety, and environmental considerations. Some additional questions and statements to be considered (Mascitelli 2004) are:

■ Can testability be improved by having a single test connection? Is there sufficient accessibility and clearance to perform required testing?

■ Can testing be made autonomous with automated alarming or signals to communicate failures? This will eliminate or at least reduce "machine watching" by production or quality assurance personnel.

■ Can quick disconnect methods be used to facilitate the testing process (e.g., pressure testing)?

■ Can reliability be improved by avoiding dissimilar metal interfaces? Are there any other sources of potential corrosion?

■ Are there any sources of potential wear (e.g., abrasion, mechanical wear, electromigration)?

■ Can stresses on components be reduced in some way (e.g., changing part orientation, reducing thermal loads, balancing mechanical loads)?

■ Can the number of interconnections be reduced, thereby improving reliability over time?

■ Avoid sharp corners, edges, points, etc. that can potentially injure assemblers or users.

■ Ensure that any components expected to require service in the future are easily accessible and removable (e.g., field replaceable units).

■ Ensure visibility of any gauges and the like that require monitoring to assure proper equipment function.

■ Access covers should be easy to open and self-supporting.

Parameter or Robust Design

Parameter Design is one of several Taguchi Techniques, developed by Genichi Taguchi (Ross, 1988). It is used to improve product quality *without* controlling or eliminating causes of variation. Simply by more fully understanding the sources of variation, a better design may be possible, without impacting product cost. The true objective of Parameter Design is to establish robustness in the design itself. Robustness means that there will be no undesirable effect on performance when variation is introduced. Variation can be introduced from within the design or can be external to the design. If robustness can be achieved in the design, it provides a low-cost means to assure product quality.

Traditional approaches try to control or eliminate causes of variation by tightening tolerances, or through the use of process control techniques during production, all of which increase costs. Traditional approaches often result in quite expensive and sometimes unnecessary actions in an attempt to control quality. Tighter tolerances, when not really needed, drive up failure costs. Still other times, more expensive materials, components, or processes are used when lower cost items can be used instead.

Consider the following example of Parameter Design and its ability to achieve robustness. An electronic circuit is required to provide a certain output voltage to another circuit. We know that the voltage is a function of transistor gain, "A" of a particular component in the circuit. However, the team decided that additional study would be needed to determine the actual transistor gain required. Several physical experiments were performed to determine which transistor gain would provide the required output voltage.

Several interesting observations were made during the experiment and additional trials were run to determine the actual variation in transistor gain from the supplier and its effect on output voltage. The results of the various experiments are provided in Figure A.5. Note the target voltage and the corresponding transistor gain, A_x. What would you think if you heard that the team went with a transistor gain of A_z? Consider the amount of variation exhibited on the output voltage side. Are you still surprised?

Transistor Gain A_z should be chosen rather than A_x, because this option substantially reduces variation in output voltage (Distribution I versus II). The average voltage is greater than the target voltage, so an adjustment is made (Distribution II moves to III). The adjustment does not contribute additional variation.

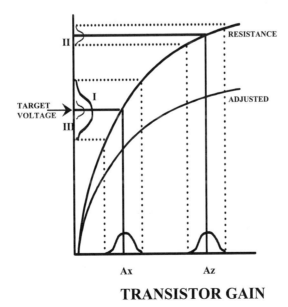

TRANSISTOR GAIN

Figure A.5

The advantage of Transistor Gain A_z is that if, for some reason, the transistor gain changes over time, the effects will not be passed on to variation in the output voltage. Many reasons for changes are possible: part variation, age, and temperature changes. Still other reasons are currently unknown to the product designers and will remain so until a failure occurs.

Traditional approaches may have led the design team to choose A_x. Then, perhaps, tighter tolerances would be imposed on the component supplied by the vendor or at assembly test (Ross 1988). What would be the result of such decisions?

Tolerance Design and the Loss Function

Tolerance Design is the traditional method used by design engineers to reduce variation. It is not the most cost-effective way to reduce variation; rather, Parameter Design is the low-cost method. Ideally, Tolerance Design should only be used after a Parameter Design study has been completed and has proven inadequate. The work performed during the Parameter Design phase will help determine the lowest cost means to conducting Tolerance Design.

The key tool used during Tolerance Design is the loss function, which provides a means to assess the economic impact of tolerances being considered. Other cost-impact estimation methods can be used, but the loss function has proven most valuable. It can also be used to substantiate the increased costs of higher quality components or tighter tolerances by estimating the impact on overall cost.

Developed by Genichi Taguchi (Ross, 1988), the loss function equation relates product variability to economic loss or cost. Taguchi realized that the cost of poor quality is not a "step function" where cost only increases when a product, part, or component is out of specification (or tolerance). Additional costs are possible even when a product, part, or component is still within specification (or tolerance). Taguchi suggested that any deviation from a target or nominal value for a part has a negative impact on product quality, cost, and even customer satisfaction.

The loss function helps to determine the impact of both offline and online quality. The equation is

$$L(y) = K [S_y2 + (Y - M)2]$$

where

S_y2 = variance attributable to the design (offline quality) determined during Parameter Design
M = target value
Y = actual value produced during the online phase
K = tolerance factor (to be covered later)

The key to tolerance design is establishing the relationship of the variance of the components or factors to the variance of the performance characteristic of interest. This is usually determined in the Parameter Design phase. The relationship between the factor variance and their contribution to the total variance in performance needs to be understood. In essence, it forces the design engineer to prioritize the parameters, determine which have the greater impact on the design, and determine which might possibly require tighter tolerances.

Total variance (S_t^2) is the summation of the individual variances as shown in:

$$s_t^2 = s_a^2 + s_b^2 + s_c^2 + \ldots\ldots$$

Let's look at the Loss Function at work, continuing our earlier electronic circuit parameter design example. The cost associated with the testing, determining an out-of-tolerance condition, documenting and to disposition the discrepancy, part replacement and reworking, and retesting an assembly is $1000. A replacement and rework must be performed if the deviation from the nominal output voltage target value exceeds 2.5 volts. For the sake of simplicity, we will consider overall variance without attempting to break down the components of variance. Therefore:

$$L(y) = K[(Y - M)^2] - \text{simplified form of Loss Function}$$

$$\$1000 = K[2.5]^2$$

$$K = \$160/v^2$$

If the current variance of transistor gain results in an output voltage *variance* of $4v^2$:

$$L(y) = \$160/v^2\ [4v^2]$$

The average loss per assembly is

$$L(y) = \$640$$

A higher-priced transistor would result in a reduction of variance to $2v^2$. The associated increase in supplier cost for testing and screening is $200 per transistor (one per assembly). Would this be a wise investment?

$$L(y) = 160\ [2v^2]$$
$$= \$320/\text{assembly} + \$200\ \text{additional cost}$$
$$= \$520/\text{assembly}$$

When compared to the $640 loss per assembly, this is a substantial reduction in loss and, therefore, is worthwhile.

If tight tolerances are placed on less influential factors, the total variance (or loss) of the product performance will not change substantially, while the overall cost has increased. Furthermore, a design engineer will need to be knowledgeable of approximate loss costs at the various levels of production and test, so that effective cost tradeoff decisions may be made. When determining tolerances, additional considerations exist. These include available process capability and part/component capabilities. These are factored into the determination of an appropriate tolerance.

The Loss Function can be used to help designers understand the relationship between tight tolerances and their impact on product quality, cost, and customer satisfaction. In this way, it can assist designers with trade-off decisions in the development process (Ross, 1988).

Design of Experiments

Design of Experiments (DOE) is a statistical technique to improve the efficiency of experimentation and to increase the effective use of the information generated through experimentation. As such, it is an important tool for the Lean product developer. It allows an experimenter to analyze multiple variables at the same time. It can even help the experimenter understand the dependency or relationships between variables.

The methodologies were originally developed in the 1890s by Robert Fisher, who was working in agriculture to improve crop yields. In the 1970s, Genichi Taguchi (Ross, 1988) developed even more efficient experiment strategies and methods.

Sometimes the relationships of variables are evident and the data are easily interpreted. This is not always the case. The information from an experiment does not always clearly dictate the action that should be taken. Often, numerical information regarding the relationships between variables is more valuable to a design engineer. The strength of the relationship can be quantified. However, experimentation takes time and money to complete. What can be done to optimize the investment? Efficient experiment strategies have been developed over the years. These experiment strategies were devised so that:

■ Optimization of the data obtained may be achieved.
■ The number of experiments performed is minimized without loss of effectiveness.
■ Interactions between variables (or "factors") may be estimated.

The experiment strategies have been devised based on the principle of orthogonality, which means that the factors in an experiment can be evaluated independently of one another. The effect of one factor does not interfere with the estimation of the effect of another factor. One provision of orthogonality is a balanced experiment, an equal number of samples under the various treatment conditions. Let us look at an example of nonorthogonality.

	Factor (A, B, C, D)				
Trial	*Factor Level (Condition 1 and 2)*				
	A	*B*	*C*	*D*	*Result*
1	1	1	1	1	XXX (Baseline)
2	2	1	1	1	XXX
3	1	2	1	1	XXX
4	1	1	2	1	XXX
5	1	1	1	2	XXX

The above example represents a traditional approach to designing an experiment. It is very common, in the traditional approach, to start with a baseline condition, changing one factor at a time to determine the effects. However, what fair comparisons can be made? Can we take the average results of all the trials under condition A_1 and compare them to the average results of all the trials under condition A_2? There is just one trial under condition A_2 and four under condition A_1. Therefore, this would *not* be a fair comparison.

Only when Trial 1 is compared to other trials, one at a time, are the factor effects orthogonal and the comparisons fair. However, this situation makes separation of any of the main factor effects impossible, let alone any interactive effects. How can this situation be overcome, while maintaining the objectives of an efficient and effective experiment strategy?

The answer is a factorial experiment strategy. A full factorial experiment is shown below:

	Factor (A, B)		
Trial	*Level (1 and 2)*		*Result*
	A	*B*	
1	1	1	XX
2	1	2	XX
3	2	1	XX
4	2	2	XX

In this experiment strategy, all possible combinations exist for the two factors and the two levels. There is an equal quantity of each. Therefore, both factor and interactive effects can be fairly estimated. However, there is a minimum of 2^f combinations that must be tested, where f is the number of factors, each at two levels. For seven factors, this would require an amazing 128 combinations. Time and financial limitations preclude the use of full factorial experiments. More efficient and economical strategies have been developed. These are called fractional factorial experiments (FFEs).

Fractional factorial experiments (½, ¼, and ⅛ FFEs) have been developed in which certain treatment conditions are chosen to maintain the orthogonality among the various factors and interactions. For example, ⅛ FFEs use only sixteen test combinations, instead of 128, for a seven-factor, two-level experiment. Taguchi has developed a family of FFE matrices (orthogonal arrays) that are even more efficient. His "L8" matrix of orthogonal array (OA) is a type of 1/16 FFE. It is shown below.

Trial	Factor (Column)						
	1	2	3	4	5	6	7
1	1	1	1	1	1	1	1
2	1	1	1	2	2	2	2
3	1	2	2	1	1	2	2
4	1	2	2	2	2	1	1
5	2	1	2	1	2	1	2
6	2	1	2	2	1	2	1
7	2	2	1	1	2	2	1
8	2	2	1	2	1	1	2

Upon close examination, one can see that orthogonality is maintained. However, remember that there is never a "free lunch." The ability to perform just eight experiments instead of 128 comes at a cost as well. More specifically, the user loses the ability to examine "higher order" interactions between factors. For example, the experiment above could not be used to examine three-way interactions or the relationships among three factors taken together.

The power of using an Orthogonal Array is the ability to evaluate several factors in a minimum number of experiments.

So far, we have discussed experiment strategies. Hopefully, you can see that these are not as complicated and time consuming as you may have initially thought. The efficient experiment strategies available can really help. But what to do with the information once it has been obtained? Some form of analysis must be performed. The most commonly used technique is an analysis of variance (ANOVA).

ANOVA is a statistically based decision tool for detecting any differences in average performance of groups of items tested. (Any basic statistics textbook can serve as a reference for ANOVA.) Other techniques exist, including analysis of means, observation, and ranking methods. The experimental designs and subsequent analysis are intrinsically tied to one another.

Process Capability Studies

In the production planning stage, it is often necessary to understand the capability of the production processes being considered. Process capability refers to the inherent ability of the process to turn out similar end products. The goal is to achieve the best distribution of output that can be maintained in statistical control for a sustained period of time, under a given set of conditions. A process capability study is a systematic procedure for determining the capability of a process by means of control charts and calculating several key measures and, if necessary, changing the process to obtain better capability.

Several key terms used within this process are

- Distribution: How the data varies and is spread out. A histogram displays the distribution of the data.
- Statistical control: Basic statistical calculations (average, standard deviation) tell us what to expect from a process. As long as we meet our expectations, we are in statistical control.
- Sustained period of time: Capability must be displayed over a sufficient amount of time, not just for a limited period.
- Given set of conditions: If conditions of the process are changed, the capability of the process will also change.

Predicting the amount of variation that processes will exhibit can be valuable to designers so that they may set realistic specification limits. If the capability of a process has been accurately determined, we can select the appropriate process for meeting specifications and tolerances. By understanding the current capability of a process, we have a basis for measuring the effects of *planned* changes that are implemented for the purpose of improving process performance. Similarly, process capability provides a basis for identifying unplanned changes to the process. Finally, it can provide a basis for establishing a schedule of periodic process control checks and planned process readjustments (e.g., preventive maintenance).

The steps of a process capability study are as follows:

1. Define the process.
2. Determine all of the process parameters. Make certain that appropriate process parameters are controlled.
3. Determine variables that will be measured and used for the study. Determine an acceptable method of measurement.
4. Collect data from the process by obtaining a series of measurements. Record all relevant information regarding the process parameters at the time the measurements are being taken.
5. Plot statistical patterns; graph histograms and control charts.
6. Interpret the patterns: calculate C_p, C_{pk}, percentage expected outside of specifications.
7. Based on the interpretations, let the patterns dictate actions to be taken.
8. Repeat steps 2 through 7 if changes are made to the process.

There are two measures of process capability:

- C_p
- C_{pk}

These standardized measures relate the variation of the process (what we can expect from the process) to the requirements the process must consistently meet (specifications, tolerances, standards). Process capability can be described by one or both of these measures. However, they describe the relationship between process variation and requirements in slightly different ways.

C_p relates process variation (the spread of the process data) as measured by the standard deviation, to the product specifications or tolerances. It is calculated as:

$$C_p = \frac{\text{Specification range}}{\text{Process Capability}} = \frac{\text{USL} - \text{LSL}}{6\,(\text{Std. Dev.})}$$

In other words, it relates the spread of the specification to the spread of the process. Six times the standard deviation is used because statistics tell us that for most normal processes, 99.73 percent of all production will fall within this range of data. C_p can be improved by reducing the standard deviation or spread of the data. Typically, the higher the C_p, the lower will be the amount of product, which is outside specification limits. A visual representation of C_p is provided in Figure A.6.

C_{pk} relates process variation to product specifications or tolerances using both the standard deviation and the average. It is calculated as:

$$C_{pk} = \text{the minimum of:} \quad \frac{(\text{Average} - \text{LSL})}{3\,(\text{Std. Dev.})}$$

$$\text{or:} \quad \frac{(\text{USL} - \text{Average})}{3\,(\text{Std. Dev.})}$$

In other words, C_{pk} relates the center of the process data to each specification limit, while taking into account the spread of the data. For this process, we choose the minimum value because this reflects the worse situation where the process data are shifted more to one side than the other. There are two ways of improving the C_{pk}: moving the average toward the center of the specification and reducing the standard deviation or spread of the data. The higher the value of C_{pk}, the lower will be the amount of product, which is outside specification limits (Western Electric, 1985). A visual representation of C_{pk} is provided in Figure A.7.

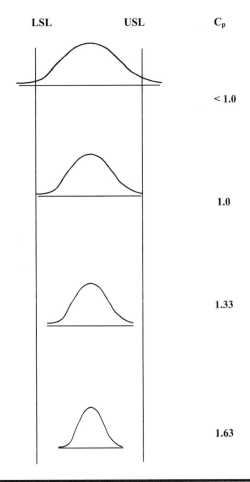

Figure A.6

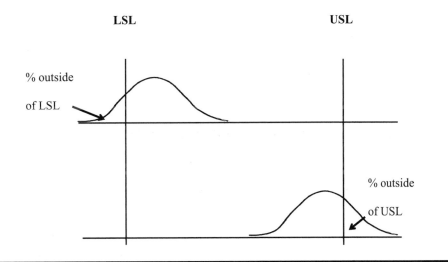

Figure A.7

Failure Mode Effect And Analysis (FMEA)

FMEA, also know as Design Failure Mode Effect and Analysis (DFMEA), is a design-review process that focuses on the proactive identification of product risks. It is a methodical way of examining a design at the system or component levels for possible ways in which failures can occur. For each potential failure, we estimate its effect on the system as well as its seriousness.

In addition, a review is made of the action or actions being planned to minimize the probability of failure or to reduce the effect of the failure. Now, it is not typically necessary to conduct the analysis of failure for every component; instead, the designer's experience is used to single out components that are critical to the operation of the product. The analysis can be used to prioritize redesign efforts, and is useful in planning for inspection, testing, assembly, maintainability, and safety.

A template can be used to help facilitate the FMEA (see below). Note that there is a ranking system for the probability of occurrence and the seriousness of the failure to the system. If desired, organizations can calculate a risk of priority number based on the probability of occurrence and seriousness ratings. Priority is then assigned to investigating failure modes with high-risk priority numbers.

Other considerations in the analysis include:

■ Safety: Injury is the most serious of all failure effects.
■ Effect on downtime: Must the system stop until repairs are made or can repairs be made during shut down (e.g., off-shift)?
■ Access: How easy is it to get to the failed component?
■ Repair planning: What is the expected repair time? What tools will be required?
■ Recommendations: What instructions should be included in operation or maintenance manuals? What changes in the design itself should be made based on this analysis?

Failure Mode Effect and Analysis Template

Product: _____ Date: _____ By: _____

Component	Possible Failure	Cause of Failure	Type of Failure	Probability of Occurrence	Serious- ness of Failure	Effect on Product	Alternatives

Notes: Type of failure = hydraulic, mechanical, wear, electrical, software. Probability of Occurrence: 1 = Very Low (<1 in 1000), 2 = Low (3 in 1000), 3 = Medium (5 in 1000), 4 = High (7 in 1000), 5 = Very High (>9 in 1000). Seriousness of failure to system: 1 = Very Low, 2 = Low, 3 = Medium, 4 = High, 5 = Very High.

Tool Summary

System Design	Techniques, Tools
1. Identify, understand, and prioritize (i.e., importance weight) customer requirements and critical to success factors.	■ Customer research, surveys, focus groups, interviews, observation
2. Determine the interrelationships between the design requirements and the manner by which they fulfill customer requirements. Determine importance values for design requirements.	■ Quality function deployment (QFD), target costing
3. Develop a set of design alternatives, periodically assess and narrow alternatives. Agree on design concept.	■ Pugh matrix ■ Set-based concurrent engineering (SBCE) ■ Target Costing ■ Design for manufacturability (DFM) ■ Production Preparation Process (3P)
4. Determine target values for each design requirement. Identify elements of the design that require more in-depth study and analysis.	■ Quality function deployment
Parameter Design	
5. State the Parameter Design problem in specific terms and determine the objective of necessary experimentation and/or study.	
6. Design an effective experiment or study by: identifying factors that influence performance characteristics, determining the measurement method and assessment criteria, selecting the appropriate test strategy.	■ Design of experiment (DOE) ■ Process capability studies
7. Conduct the experiment or study and analyze the data, interpret results, determine most influential factors, select optimum parameter values for the most influential parameters, run a confirmation experiment or study.	■ Analysis of variance (ANOVA) ■ Observation methods ■ Process capability studies ■ Design of experiment (DOE)
8. Determine if product performance will adequately fulfill customer requirements. If not, those corresponding parameters will need additional study in the Tolerance Design phase.	■ Failure mode effect and analysis (FMEA)

System Design	*Techniques, Tools*
Tolerance Design	
9. Use Tolerance Design techniques on the most influential parameters to control product performance in order to assure that the design fulfills customer requirements.	■ Loss function ■ Design for manufacturability (DFM) ■ Failure mode effect and analysis (FMEA) ■ Process capability studies

Reference

Juran, J.M. and Gryna, F. (1993) *Quality Planning and Analysis*, McGraw Hill, New York.

King, B. (1989) *Better Designs in Half the Time*, GOAL/QPC, Methuen, MA.

Mascitelli, R. (2004) *The Lean Design Guidebook*, Technology Perspectives. The guidebook provides numerous and specific "design for manufacturability" examples, many were listed.

Ross, P. (1988) *Taguchi Techniques for Quality Engineering*, McGraw Hill, New York.

Ward, A. and Sobek, D. (1996) Principles from Toyota's set based concurrent engineering process, *Proceedings of the 1996 ASME Design Engineering Technical Conference*, Irvine, CA.

Western Electric (1985) *Statistical Quality Control Handbook*, Delmar Printing, Delmar, NY. This is the "grandfather" of all SQC books originally printed in 1956.

Index

Page numbers in italics refer to figures

A

ANOVA, *see* analysis of variance
available time, 27

B

batching, 10, 11, 26, *see also* design process
variability
 and design process, 28
 impact on flow, 11, 28, 66, 68
batch size
 comparison among batch, queue, and flow
 processing, 65–70
 elements of, 26, 28–29, 72
 illustration, *66*
bill of material (BOM), 11, 12, *25*, 27,
 28, 39, 45
BOM, *see* bill of material

C

Complete Lean Enterprise, 1
concurrent (simultaneous) engineering, 47,
 48–49, 50
 vs. sequential, *47, 69, see also* lean
 principles
Cooper, Robert, 48
critical management tasks, 1
customer viewpoint, importance of, 5, 15, 20,
 24, 52, 55, 72, 100

D

data box, 10, 11, 24, *25*, 30, 37
data distribution, 116
DFM, *see* design for manufacturability
DFMEA, *see* design for manufacturability
DPCSM, *see* development process's current
 state map
design of experiments (DOE), 47
 analysis of variance (ANOVA), 115
 efficient experiment strategies, 114–116
 and lean product, 113
 traditional vs. factorial experiments,
 115–116
design for manufacturability (DFM)
 changes in, 104–105, 114
 considerations of testability, safety, and
 environment, 110
 cost accountability, 107
 design firm partner training, 86
 electrical design elements, evaluating, 109
 key principles of, 105, 107
 mechanical design elements, questioning
 of, 108–109
 prototype, 79–81
 product reliability, 110
 software design and hardware
 interface, 110
 and value engineering, 107–108
 See also Pugh matrix; SBCE
design for manufacturability and assembly
 (DFMA), *see* design for manufacturability
 (DFM)
design requirements, relationship matrix, 100
development process
 cost modeling, 97–99
 customer impact on, 13, *see also* quality
 function deployment, 99–100
 lead time, 24, 27–28
 observation of, 27

and power of value stream mapping, 9, 88
process time (touch time), 27
employing quality metric, 29
regulatory limitations on, 13
resource management, 6
sequential process of, 47
task orientation, 45
variability in, 6, 9–10, 11–12
volume of transactions, 30–31
development process's current state map
(DPCSM)
completion time, 25
customer needs, *24*
obtaining critical data, 26
root causes, 9, 10, 30
suggested steps for assessment, 23–25,
26–30
visual depiction, 23
walking the flow, 30
development waste
calculating, 18
categories of, 15–16
"eyes for flow" and "eyes for waste," 9, 12,
15, 24
identifying, 12, 13, 21, 26–27, 48
reducing, 26, 27, 49, 80
terms defined, 15
DevelopTek's Future State, 77–83, *84*, 87–88;
See also lean thinking
DevelopTek Value Stream Mapping
Project, *7*, 32
calculating value stream summary metrics,
42–43
as case study, 35, 37–44, application for
design, 77–81
customer needs, 36, 77
current state map, 35, *36*, 37–44, *80*
development process, review and
evaluation of, 35, 37
first pass yield (FPY) calculation, *43*, 44, 52
future state map, *79, 80–81*
initial specifications, 38
and implementation *82–83*
potential interruptions, 81, 82–83
process time, 42
and reduction of 85, 88
prototype, building, testing, redesign,
38–42
recommendations, 81, *82–83*
suppliers and lead time, 41, 85
value stream summary metrics, *42–43*, 44
verification and supplementing of
data, *40–41*
DOE, *see* design of experiments

E

Enterprise Resource System (ERP), 39
ERP, *see* enterprise resource system

F

FAA, *see* Federal Aviation Administration
FDA, *see* Federal Drug Administration
failure mode effect and analysis (FMEA)
analytical consideration of
failure, 120
design-review process, 120
minimizing failure, *119*
template for, 120
families (product or service), 4–5
application of information, 4
and product or service, 5, 9
reapplication of information, 4, 6
work content, 5
FDA, *see* Federal Drug Administration
Federal Aviation Administration (FAA), 72
Federal Drug Administration (FDA), 72
FEEs, *see* fractional factorial experiments
FIFO, *see* first-in-first-out lanes
first-in-first-out lanes (FIFO), 71, 74,
75, *84–85*
first pass yield (FPY) and first time
quality, 18, 44, 52
Fisher, Robert, 114
FMEA, *see* failure mode effect and analysis
FPY, *see* first pass yield
fractional factorial experiments (FFEs)
family of FFE matrices and
streamlining, 116
See also orthogonal array
Future State Map
achievement based on lean
concepts, 55, 75, 89
checklists, 6, 18, 51, 65, 89
cost modeling, 58
and unlevel demands, *74*, 89,
97, 98–99
creation of, 55, 59
customer needs, 4
VOC, 20, 55, 57, *58*, 89
designing, 26, 56–57, 61, 76
and standards, 90–91
guidelines (questions), 55, 56
service/output, 57–58, 89–93
implementation of, 2, 56 73–74,
89, 92–94

information quality, 7, 18, 64–65
   and improved communication among
     functions, 66
   iterations and icons, 28, 56
   lean notes and examples, 49, 61, 62, 64,
     67–68, 67–72, 73, 74, 75
   perceived value of improvement, 57–58
     fast track, 75
   minimizing root causes, 9, 21, 55,
     59, 64, 65
   prioritizing work, 85–87
   resource allocation, 67
     basic pull systems, 71
   service level consistency, 58, 59
   streamlining, 27, 59, 61, 62, *74*
   summary measures, 88
   suppliers, 49, 52, 59–60
gemba (workplace), 30, 63

H

House of Quality
   design requirements, *100*
   product features, 101
   and voice of customer, *101*, 103

I

inbox icon, *29–30*, 32
information quality, 10–11, 15–16, 18
inventory (or queues), 26, 29–30, *see* also
  batching
iteration icon, 11, 28
iterations, good vs. bad, 50–51

J

Jones, Daniel, 1

K

kaizen burst icon, 56, 75–76, 88
kentou phase, 50
Keyte, Beau, 1
knowledge creation, 6, 46–47
knowledge, reusue of, 4, 6, 45–46

L

lead time, 11, 13, 25, 26, *27, 28, 32,* 37, 48, 58
Lean Development Principles, 1, 5, *see also*
  Future State
   concurrent nature of, *49*
   efficiency assessment, 45–53, 64–66
   key concepts, 45, 52, 56, 73
   knowledge reuse and design libraries,
     45–46
   illustrated, 52
   one piece flow, 69–70
     prioritization of work, 70
    process performance vs. lessons learned,
     51, 66, 74
   tools, 52, 120–121
   traditional vs. lean, 45–50, 62
lean notes and examples, 5, 6, 16, 19, 20, 21,
  31, 46, 48, 50, 52, 59, 64
lean practioner, 12
lean thinking
   assessing current state, 2, 9, 11, 12
   behavioral changes, 96
   focus, 51
   and *gemba*, 30–31
   lead time goals,12, 58–60, 63–64
   learning opportunities, 73
   leveling volume of work, 74
   obstacles to, 49
   process of, 2, 50
   results-oriented design of future
     state, 2, 9
   service matrix, 6
Lean Thinking, 1
Learning to See, 1
Liker, Jeff, 50, 69
Locher, Drew, 1
loops, 10, and information quality issues,
  10–11, 92–94, 94

M

management timeframe (pitch)
   frequency of review, 63, 79
   traditional vs. lean, 62
mapping team
   composition of, 6, 33
   cross–functional participants, 2
   design production and kaizen burst icon,
     56–57, 76, 81–83
   devopment of shared vision, 2
   guidelines for, 2–3

implementation plan, 92–93
inclusion of suppliers, customers, and engineers, 6, 73
onsite review and recommendations, 23–33, 78
problem resolution at workplace, 63
responsibilities of, 6, 13, 30–32, 63, 95
mapping tips
  clarifying scope, key questions, 3
  frequency of review, 63
  closed loop format, 37
  data collection process, 26
  estimating resource allocation, 10
  identifying key improvement projects, 56
  frequency of review, 63
  information quality, 11
  kaizen burst icon, usefulness of, 52
  mapping team/ value stream mapping event, 33
  narrowing icon, 50
  prioritizing development projects, 111
  productive value stream mapping event, 2–3
  reevaluation of value stream summary measures, 44
  simplicity in/of design, 13
MDTs, *see* module development teams
module development teams (MDTs), 50
Morgan, James, 50, 69

N

Nakao, Chichiro, 105
nonvalue added processing waste (or overprocessing), 16, 18, 19–20, 80

O

OA, *see* orthogonal array
Ono, Taiichi, 15
One-piece flow, *69, 70*
orthogonal array (OA)
  Taguchi's L8 matrix illustrated, 116
  usefulness of, 116
outside resource icon, 24

P

parameter design
  comparing factor variance and total variance, 113

robustness and product quality, 110–111
pockets of flow, 69
  first-in-first-out (FIFO) lanes, *71*
  queue management and, *70*
problem solving, 1, 85–87
process box, 10
process capability study
  critical steps of, 116–118
  defined, 116
  and standard deviation, 118, *119*
process quality metric, 29, 30, 37
process time, 25, 31
product (service) matrix, 4
production prototype, 13, 47
  and design freeze, 47–48
production systems, types of, 71, 73
Pugh Matrix (criteria–based matrix)
  application of, 103
  basic template, 103
  convergence of alternative concepts, 104
  critical-to-success factors, 103
  qualitative comparisons, 100–101

Q

QFD, *see* quality function deployment
quality function deployment (QFD)
  implementation in product and process development, *102*
  and customer driven prioritization, 99, 101
  Mitsubishi model, 99

R

rapid product prototyping, 47, 49, 50
Rother, Mike, 1

S

SBCE, *see* set-based concurrent engineering
set-based concurrent engineering (SBCE)
  application of, 104–105
  benefit of collaborative design, 105
  defined, 104
  principles of, 105
Shook, John, 1
SIPOC, *see* supplier input-process-output-customer scoping document
Sobek, D., 53

stage gates, 48
streamlining time to market, 2, 26
supplier-input-process-output-customer
  scoping document (SIPOC), 6, 23, example
  of, 7
system and parametric design, 47

T

Taguchi, Genichi, 110, 111, 114
Taguchi Techniques, 110–111
Takt time (internal of time)
    application, 60–62, 74, 78
    compared to process time, 61, 86
    defined, *60*
    Takt image, 63
target costing, 97
    key elements of, 97–98
    and product cost drivers, 98–99
    timing calculations, 97
tolerance design
    defined, 112
    cost impact and loss function, 112–113
    rapid prototype, 106
tool summary, 121–122
Toyota, lessons learned, 15, 52, 68, 69, 70, 99,
  104, 106
Toyota Production Development System, 50
"3P" (Production Preparation Process)
    and concurrent design, *106*
    cross-functional involvement, 106
    outlined, 106
trystorming, 46–47, *see* brainstorming

V

value stream, 1
value stream mapping

application to development
  process, 4–5, 13
application to manufacturing, 1, 25,
  30–31, 50
defined, 1, 23
information management, 1, *7*, 30–31
in-scope, 4, 7, 8
implementation of, 2, 32, 56, 57
objectives, 7–8, 12
out-of-scope, 6, 8, 25
mapping process, *2, 4,* 7
pull processing, 70–71
simplicity vs. "swim lanes" *12*, 13
summary metrics, 32
walking the flow, 19, 30–32
value stream mapping event (VSM),
  2–3, 30–31
    key questions, 3
    learning opportunities, *93*
    logistical planning, 3, and virtual
      tour, 31–32
    preparation for, 3, 6, 21
    project plan, 8, 23
    report out, timing of, *93–94*
value stream mapping tool (VSMT), 9
value stream summary measures, 32
value stream team manager, 2
    assessment by, 52
    guidelines for, 3–4, 33
    management skills required, 95, 96
VOC, *see* voice of customer
voice of customer (VOC), 19, *81, 83, 84, 92,*
  94, 103
VSM, *see* value stream mapping event
VSMT, *see* value stream mapping tool

W

Ward, Allen, 50, 104
Womak, James, 1